re the
vil'

RUSTIE LEE
A Taste of the Caribbean

HandE Publishers
LONDON

Published by HandE Publishers Ltd
Epping Film Studios, Brickfield Business Centre
Thornwood High Road, Epping CM16 6TH
www.handepublishers.co.uk

First published in the United Kingdom in 2007
Second Edition 2009

ISBN 978-0-9548518-8-0

A CIP catalogue record for this book is available from
The British Library

Edited by Kayleigh Hart, Natalie-Jane Revell & Meia Arnold
Page design, typesetting and photography by Dave Palmer
Cover design by Ruth Mahoney

Printed and bound in 2009 by ORYMU Artes Gráficas
Ruiz de Alda 1, 28320 Pinto, Madrid, Spain

Location: San Souci couples resort, Jamaica
and Epping Film Studios
Set design by Lathams of Epping

Contents

Introduction

I moved to England with my family when I was 5 years old.
It was my Mother who inspired me as she was always busy in the
kitchen so I grew up to enjoy great food. I have sampled dishes
from all over the world and needless to say ... I LOVE FOOD!
Growing up in a Caribbean household was different, yet exciting;
however, at the time it was difficult to find tropical food, which
thankfully has now changed.

My parents would get very excited when they heard of a shop that
sold foods, such as mangoes, yams and plantains.
People would travel for miles to get hold of these products, which
is so different from today, where you can find most of these items
in the local supermarkets.

I am sure there are recipes in this book that you will enjoy and come back to time and time again.

The array of smells that each dish gives off are mouth-watering and I hope that you will cook and enjoy them for yourselves.

I went back to Jamaica, not only to show you a part of the Caribbean that these dishes are traditional from, but to show you how wonderfully simple foods can be.

I hope this will encourage you to try new delights and not be scared to add something different to your shopping list.

All that leaves me to say is 'Good Nammings', which means 'good eating and enjoy'.

Utensils

Utensils

Utensils

It is always good to have a kitchen full of useful utensils to help assist you and achieve a high standard of culinary delights.

A good set of knives is virtually paramount; a cheap set won't last you that long and will make work difficult.

Make sure you have an assorted arrangement of spoons, including lattice spoons for draining and different sized ladles for small to large portions.

A variety of pots, pans, saucepans and griddle pans will also come into great use.

Make sure you have a good collection of chopping boards and baking trays.

It is also a good idea to have a food processor and an electric whisk for quickness.

Storage Jars

These should be sterilized by either boiling the jars or a sterilizing product which will give you instructions on how to carry out the sterilization process.

Dutchie Pot

A Dutchie pot is a large, heavy, round cooking pot with a close-fitting lid.

They can come in various sizes, similar to our saucepans.

The pot is made of cast iron and can be used either in the oven or on the hob.

They are traditionally used in Jamaica and other Caribbean cultures for braising meat, making soups and similar dishes.

Herbs & Spices

Chilli

Chillies add a marvellous pungency to Caribbean cookery and are a staple ingredient of many dishes.
The pods range in colour and strength; a good rule is, the smaller, darker and more pointed the chilli is, the hotter it will be.
Chilli can be used fresh or in powder form.
If using fresh, cut the pods in half and brush out the seeds and remove the pith inside, being careful when handling them.

Cinnamon

This grows on a tree which is a member of the Laurel family and has a sweet, musky flavour.
If you can, buy cinnamon in shavings as it keeps better.
Alternatively, it can also come in sticks or grounded.

Ginger

The West Indies are reputed to grow the best ginger, which can be used dried, fresh, ground or preserved.
It can be used in almost all types of cooking and is a great aid to digestion.

Mace

Is the aromatic, lacy outer covering of the nutmeg, but smells and tastes much stronger.
It can be bought as whole, 'blade' mace or ground and is used in most recipes for sweets or seasoning vegetables.

Nutmeg

This is the dark brown nut or 'stone' which is inside the mace covering.
It is sold whole or ground, but its scent diminishes very quickly.
Nutmeg can be used in most foods and is a great aid to digestion.

Saffron

Is derived from the crocus and produces a full range of yellow and orange shades and has a spicy, slightly bitter taste. A little saffron goes a long way.

Pimento

Is also known as Allspice, as its berries smell like a blend of cinnamon, cloves and nutmeg.
It is used whole for marinades, pickles and chutneys, or ground for cakes and puddings.

Vegetables

Aubergine (eggplant)

This is also known as eggplant as there is a variety which produces fruit exactly the size, colour and shape of an egg.

The most familiar variety is the large, tapered, deep purple type.

Unless being used in salads, they should not be peeled as the skin provides flavour and holds the flesh together.

Coco or Eddo

A hairy root about the size of a large potato, although taste's more starchy.

Pink or white in colour, they can be boiled until tender.

Callaloo

Is a leafy-spinach type plant, commonly used in soups.

It is not usually available in Britain as a fresh vegetable, but is now appearing in tins in some supermarkets.

Cho-Cho

This is a pear-shaped member of the melon family.

There are several types ranging in appearance, size and colour.

They are eaten cooked and can be a substitute for any marrow recipe.

Peeled and thinly sliced and the core removed, they need boiling for roughly 10 minutes to be tender.

Scotch Bonnet

This is a variety of the chilli pepper and is one of the hottest peppers in the world.

These peppers are used to flavour a variety of dishes and is what gives Jerk and other Caribbean dishes their unique flavours.

Congo, Gungoo or Gungo (peas)

They grow on bushes and require about 35 minutes of boiling to make them tender.

What Jamaicans call peas are known in Britain as red kidney beans.

Worth remembering if you go to a Jamaican shop.

Fruit

Paw-Paw or Papaya

From the outside they appear like a green hand-grenade and not particularly inviting.
Cut one open and you see beautiful golden coloured flesh and a centre of tiny black seeds,
which should be scraped out before eating.

Mango

One of the most popular of the tropical fruits, with a delicate fragrance and a slightly 'spicy' taste.
If using immediately, then chose the ones that are softer to the touch and of a yellow-reddish colour.

Guava

Is a small yellow skinned fruit, with yellow/pink flesh, lots of seeds and a musky odour.
They can be eaten raw or cooked and are best made into jelly or jam.

Ugli

Appears to look more like a lumpy grapefruit, but tastes like a cross between a tangerine
and grapefruit, but sweeter.
It can be used as an alternative in any recipe that specifies oranges.

Watermelon

This is a lovely refreshing fruit as it contains about ninety percent water.
A ripe watermelon should sound dull and flat when you thump it and the skin should ideally
be dark green.

Fruit

Banana

Of course we all know what a banana looks and tastes like, but we often make the mistake of using the fruit before it is fully ripe.

A light sprinkling of brown speckles on the skin is the sign of ripeness and does not mean the fruit is going bad, the more speckled the skin, the better the fruit will taste inside.

Green bananas can be boiled as part of a main course meal.

Plantain

This is a member of the banana family and is only eaten cooked.

They resemble bananas but are generally sold individually rather than in bunches.

Plantains go well in soups, stews and as a dessert and they can be cooked any way you chose.

Pineapple

A ripe fresh pineapple will be fragrant and juicy and will 'give' slightly under pressure.

When preparing, the long woody core should be removed as this is inedible.

They can be eaten raw or cooked.

Coconut

This is a very versatile fruit as all of it can be used.

To open, pierce two of its brown 'eyes', strike with a hammer and break the shell open to expose the creamy white meat, which can be shredded or grated.

Dips, Sauces
&
Spice

In this section of the book I want to try and tempt you into having a go at making your own accompaniments instead of buying them off the shelves.

Nowadays, it's so convenient to purchase and store these products, but in reality it is just as easy to buy the ingredients and make more for less.

It is amazing how a little of something can add so much flavour to your food.
For example, the scotch bonnet pepper is a traditional, Caribbean ingredient used for spicing up dishes but beware it's very HOT!

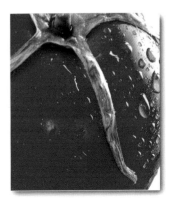

Kick-y Butter

Method

Boil the chives, parsley and garlic in water for 5 minutes then strain.

Blend the herbs with the butter and season to taste.

On a board, roll the mixture into a 1 inch roll with the hands.

Wrap in wet greaseproof paper and chill in the refrigerator.

Ingredients

1 tsp chopped chives
1 tsp chopped parsley
2 cloves chopped garlic
4 ½ tbsp hot water
75g (3oz) butter
Salt and pepper to season
Greaseproof paper

Avocado Dip

Method

Cut each avocado in half, lengthways and remove the stone.

Scoop out the flesh into a bowl and mash to a paste.

Add the remaining ingredients, except the paprika, and blend well.

Cover with cling film and chill in the refrigerator.

On serving, sprinkle with paprika.

Ingredients

2 large avocado pears
1 tsp onion, grated
2 tsp lime or lemon juice
4 tbsp mayonnaise
Pinch of white pepper
Pinch of salt
Paprika for garnish

Tomato Chutney
Method

Chop the tomatoes, onions and apples.

Place in a deep bowl with all of the other ingredients.

Pressure cook in small amounts, then combine the ingredients in a large, heavy saucepan.

Bring to the boil and simmer for 2-3 hours.

If you do not have a pressure cooker, this can be cooked on the hob instead.

Put into sterilized jars or bottles while warm and ensure they are closed tightly.

Ingredients

5lb tomatoes
3lb apples, peeled
2lb (900g) brown sugar
1lb (450g) raisins
6 large onions
2pts vinegar
110g (4oz) salt
15g white pepper
15g cloves
2-3 chillies, de-seeded and chopped
Peel of 3 lemons, sliced

Mint Chutney
Method

Mince all ingredients, with the exception of the mustard and salt.

Put into a large pan with 200mls (7fl oz) of the vinegar.

Bring to the boil and simmer for 20-25 minutes.

Mix the remaining vinegar with the mustard and salt.

Stir into the chutney and bring to the boil once more.

Take from the heat and allow to cool.

When cold, pour into sterilized pots and tie down well.

This is delicious with various meats, but especially lamb.

Ingredients

275mls (½pt) measure filled with pressed down mint leaves
2 small onions
2 medium cooking apples, cored
225g (8oz) raisins or sultanas
110g (4oz) green or red tomatoes, skinned
225g (8oz) soft brown sugar
275mls (½pt) red wine vinegar
1 tsp dry mustard
1 tsp salt

Salsa

Method

Approximate preparation time 20 minutes

Peel the mango and tomato and finely chop the shallot, garlic, green pepper, scotch bonnet and coriander.

In a bowl, mix together the olive oil, balsamic vinegar and salt.

Add all the ingredients into the oil mixture and stir.

Put in a covered container in the refrigerator until ready to use.

Ingredients

1 large ripe mango
1 shallot
1 beef tomato
1 garlic clove, finely chopped
½ green pepper
1 bunch coriander
½ scotch bonnet
2 tsp salt
6 tbsp virgin olive oil
1 tbsp balsamic vinegar

Mango Chutney
Method

Approximate cooking time 20 minutes

Wash and peel the mangoes.

Cut the cheeks of the mango into six pieces per cheek.

Chop the garlic, onions, ginger, and scotch bonnet pepper.

Put the Dutchie pot on the heat, and place in the entire dry ingredients into it.

Stir the ingredients around; you will hear the mustard seeds pop.

Add the vinegar and bring to the boil.

Then add the brown sugar stirring until it has dissolved.

Add the mangoes, garlic, onions and simmer for 10 minutes.

Put the cooked chutney into the sterilized jars, allowing to cool a little.

Screw the tops on and allow to stand for a week.

This is a delicious chutney, tasty and hot.

Ingredients

5 green mangoes
1tbs mustard seeds
2 scotch bonnet pepper
4 ozs (100g) soft brown sugar
1 oz (25g) pimento seeds crushed
(or picking spices)
1 oz (25g) root ginger
1 oz (25g) salt
½ pt malt vinegar
1 garlic clove
1 large onion
4 x 500g jars

Guava Jam

Ingredients

3lbs ripe guavas
1lb (8oz) demerara sugar
1 ½ litres water

Method

Approximate cooking time 2 hours 30 minutes

Wash the guavas, cut the stems from the top and cut the little hard part at the bottom off.

Slice the guavas in half and then cut into thirds.

Place them in a Dutchie pot or a heavy-bottomed saucepan.

Pour the sugar over the guavas and stir in.

Add the water, place on a high heat and allow to come to the boil.

Stir occasionally with a wooden spoon.

After 5 minutes on the high heat, turn the heat down and allow to simmer.

There will be excess foam which you will need to scoop out and discard.

During the cooking, you will need to scrape down the side of the pan about every ten minutes.

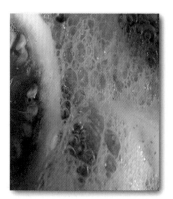

After cooking, remove from the heat.

Sieve the mixture through a fine sieve and press through as much of the fruit as possible into a metal bowl.

Return the liquid to the Dutchie pot and cook on a low heat for approximately 1½ to 2 hours.

It is ideal to use a sugar thermometer to determine the right temperature for the jam to reach, which should be about 110°C.

Lazy Days Jerk Sauce

Method

In a food processor, add everything and blend until smooth.

You may increase the amount of garlic as well as chilli peppers, according to taste.

This recipe doubles and triples well.

For use on fish, marinate overnight and simply grill.

Ingredients

2 bunches spring onions
1 tsp cinnamon
½ tsp nutmeg
1 tsp ground allspice
2 tsp soy sauce
2 tbsp brown sugar
6 garlic cloves
2 scotch bonnet peppers
1 tbsp ground thyme or 2 tbsp thyme leaves

Hot Pepper Sauce

Method

Liquidize all the ingredients together.

Bring to the boil in a small enamel or stainless steel saucepan.

Cook gently for 8-10 minutes stirring continuously

Ingredients

4tsp chilli peppers, finely chopped
3 cloves garlic, finely chopped
2 small onions, finely chopped
3 ½ tbsp malt vinegar
1 tsp salt
4 tbsp water
1 dsp olive oil

Lazy Days Jerk Seasoning
Method

Mix all ingredients together except the vegetable oil.

Place in a blender to get a rough chop until they are all combined, then add the oil a bit at a time.

Your Jerk Seasoning is now ready!

Ingredients

1 dsp all spice
1 dsp chilli powder
1 dsp paprika
2 tsp cinnamon
1 dsp salt
1 scotch bonnet pepper
½ red pepper, chopped
½ green pepper, chopped
1 bay leaf
1 medium onion, chopped
6 cloves garlic
6 fl oz vegetable oil

Curry Powder
Method

First add the cumin with the coriander, poppy and mustard seeds to a non-stick pan.

Put the oven on a medium heat and toast until the mustard seeds start to jump around.

Add the cloves and pepper and mix together.

Remove from the heat and grind the mixture with a food processor, a blender or pestle and mortar.

Mix well with the turmeric and ginger.

Use a fine sieve to place the mixture through.

Store it in a covered glass jar.

Ingredients

1 tbsp poppy seeds
1 tbsp peppercorns
2 tbsp cumin seeds
1 tbsp whole cloves
1 tbsp coriander seeds
2 tbsp ground turmeric
1 tbsp mustard seeds, brown
are preferred
1 tbsp ground ginger
(Jamaican if available)

Hunters Sauce

Method

Mix the flour and the butter to a smooth paste.

Mix the orange juice and water together in a jug.

Pour a small amount into a saucepan.

Drop little balls of the flour/butter mixture into the saucepan and, stirring all of the time, continue until all of the mixture and the liquids are used up.

Season with salt and pepper.

Then add in the cayenne pepper and the grated rind.

Stirring continuously, simmer over a low heat for 5 minutes.

Add the redcurrant jelly and cook until it melts.

Just before serving, add the rum.

This is a tangy sauce which goes really well with game or turkey.

Ingredients

25g (1oz) plain flour
25g (1oz) butter
150ml (¼ pt) orange juice
150ml (¼ pt) water
1 tsp cayenne pepper
rind and juice of 1 orange
1½ tbsp redcurrant jelly
2 tbsp rum
Salt and pepper

Spicy Tomato Sauce

Method

Sweat off onions in a large, heavy pan until golden.

Add the garlic, peppers, coriander, oregano, salt and pepper.

Cook for 5-10 minutes over a moderate heat, stirring continuously until soft but not brown.

Add chopped tomatoes, cover the pan tightly and simmer for 30-35 minutes, stirring occasionally.

Pour the sauce into a large container and allow to cool.

Blend until smooth and store in the refrigerator.

This will keep for up to 2 weeks if kept in a tightly-sealed container.

Ingredients

1 dsp vegetable oil
175g (6oz) onions
2 medium-sized peppers, seeds and pith removed and finely chopped
700g (1½lb) large tomatoes, peeled, de-seeded and chopped
2 cloves garlic, finely chopped
2 tsp coriander
1 tsp oregano
1 tsp salt
1 tsp fresh ground black pepper

Creole Sauce

Method

Heat the butter in a heavy pan.

Add all the ingredients and, stirring continuously, cook over a medium heat for 15-20 minutes.

Serve this sauce over meat, fish or poultry.

Ingredients

2 tbsp butter
1 x 400g (14oz) tin tomato soup
110mls (4fl oz) water
½ small green pepper, chopped
1 small onion, chopped
8 stuffed olives, chopped
1 tsp salt

Barbecue Sauce for Steak

Method

Put all ingredients into a saucepan and mix well.

Cook over a low heat for 15 minutes, stirring continuously.

Brush on steaks and spareribs for barbecues or grills.

Refrigerated, it will keep for a week.

Ingredients

150mls (¼pt) vegetable oil
3 tbsp vinegar
275mls (½pt) boiling water
2 tbsp worcester sauce
2 small onions, chopped
2 chillies, de-seeded and finely chopped
2 cloves garlic, grated
1 tbsp brown sugar
2 tsp salt
1 tsp French mustard
1 tsp paprika
1 tsp thyme
1 tsp sage
Bunch of parsley, finely chopped
Bunch of chives, finely chopped
Dash of tabasco sauce

Appetizers
&
Soups

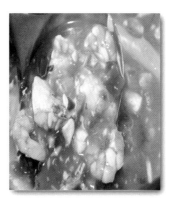

Stuffed Avocados

Method

Approximate preparation time 15 minutes

Mix together the flaked tuna fish or prawns with the onion, garlic, cucumber, parsley and mayonnaise.

Halve the avocados, remove the stones, and brush the exposed flesh with lime juice to stop discolouration.

Fill the hollows with the tuna fish mixture, serve on a bed of lettuce and tomato, and garnish with parsley.

Ingredients

4 avocados
1 x 225g (8oz) tin tuna fish
or prawns
1 small onion, finely chopped
1 clove garlic, crushed
¼ cucumber, finely chopped
Few sprigs of parsley, finely
chopped
4 tbsp mayonnaise
Juice of 1 lime
Lettuce, tomato and extra
Parsley for garnish

Prawns in melon

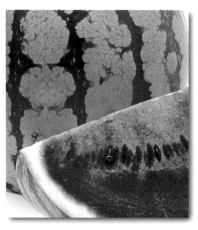

Method

Approximate preparation time 30 minutes

Slice the top off the melon. Scoop out the seeds and the flesh.

Put the 'shell' and the prawns into the refrigerator to chill.

Mix the tomato ketchup, cream, mayonnaise and chopped pepper together, and season with salt and pepper.

Cut the melon flesh into cubes and add to the sauce.

Chill, then mix the prawns and fill the melon shell.

Ingredients

1 medium-sized watermelon
175g (6oz) peeled prawns
6 tbsp mayonnaise
5 tbsp single cream
2 tbsp tomato ketchup
1 small green pepper, de-seeded and chopped
Salt and pepper
Parsley for garnish

Warm Mango, Guava & Goat's Cheese Salad

Method

Approximate preparation time 20 – 30 minutes

Peel and cut the cheeks off the mango and using a small round cutter, cut 2 circular disks.

Slice the guava into 4 rounds.

Slice the goat's cheese through the centre, maintaining the round circles.

Place the goat's cheese, guava and mangoes on a greased tray.

Brush the guava with a little oil.

Roughly chop the mixed salad and put in a bowl.

Sprinkle 1 tbsp of the pine nuts, add the sliced onion and chopped cucumber.

Sprinkle 2 tbsp of Rustie's Salad Dressing and gently mix together (see below).

Place the salad on a plate and make a heap in the centre.

Wrap the cucumber slice around the salad.

Now return to the goat's cheese and put 2 tsp of your favourite honey over the goat's cheese.

Place the tray with the mango, guava and goat's cheese under the grill for 3 minutes.

Decorate the salad by putting the goat's cheese on top of the salad, the guava disks on top showing a little of the goat's cheese and the mango on top of this.

Sprinkle with Rustie's Salad Dressing and the remaining pine nuts around the plate.

For the Salad Dressing:

In a bowl, place the paprika, salt, mustard and honey.

Mix together with a tbsp of vinegar.

Gently whisk in the olive oil and the rest of the vinegar.

Ingredients

4oz goat's cheese
1 mango
1 guava
2 tbsp honey
2 sprigs of parsley
(save one for decoration)
2 tbsp pine nuts
2 good handfuls of mixed salad
2x10 inch slices of cucumber
(use approx. 1 inch chopped in the salad)
1 medium onion, sliced

Salad Dressing

1 tbsp olive oil
1 tbsp white wine vinegar
3 tsp Dijon mustard
1 tsp paprika
1 tbsp honey
1 tsp salt

Cuttlefish Starter

Method

Approximate cooking time 20 - 25 minutes

Ask your fishmonger to clean the fish for you.

Wash thoroughly, peel away the outer skin and discard.

Cut the fish into ¼ inch strips and fry gently in the olive oil until tender.

Add the garlic, pepper, chilli powder, tomatoes and sweetcorn and cook for about 15 to 20 minutes and then add the wine, salt and pepper to taste.

Then cook for a further 5 minutes.

Ingredients

1.4kg (2lb) cuttlefish
1x400g (14oz) tin tomatoes
350g (12oz) sweetcorn
2 cloves garlic, chopped
½ medium red pepper,
de-seeded and chopped
3 tbsp olive oil
2 tsp chilli powder
1 glass white wine
Salt and pepper to season

Fish Pancakes

Ingredients

For the Pancakes:
175g (6 oz) plain flour
2 large eggs
275mls (½ pint milk)
1 tsp salt
Oil for frying

For the Sauce:
25g (1oz) plain flour
25g (1oz) butter
275ml (½ pt) milk
8 oz of tin chopped tomatoes
½ tsp salt
½ tsp pepper

For the Filling:
450g (1lb) white fish, cooked and flaked
175g (6oz) shrimps
1 large onion
2 tomatoes, chopped
1 tsp chilli powder
1tsp salt
Oil for frying
1 tsp pepper

8 Large cooked prawns for decoration
2 Sprigs parsley, chopped
(save some for decoration)

Method

Approximate cooking time 20 – 30 minutes

For the pancakes:

Sieve the flour into a bowl.
Make a well in the centre and add the egg.
Slowly add the milk, season with the salt and mix to a smooth batter.
Leave to stand for 10 minutes.
Heat the oil in a heavy pan and fry the pancakes, using enough batter just to cover the base of the pan.
Remember to toss them with care!
Place on a plate to cool.

To make the sauce for the filling:

Mix the flour and butter together in a bowl.
Place the milk onto the hob, medium heat, and when the milk is hot gradually add the flour/butter mixture.
Keep stirring until the mixture thickens.
Add the chopped tin tomatoes, parsley, salt and pepper to your sauce mixture and stir in and cook for a further 2 minutes.
(Save a little sauce to pour over the pancakes.)

For the filling:

Heat the oil and sweat the onions for 3 - 4 minutes and then add your fish, shrimps, fresh chopped tomatoes, chilli powder, salt and pepper and cook for a further 2 - 3 minutes and stir.
Add the sauce to your fish mixture gently combining the two mixtures together.
Put 3tbls of the fish mixture into each pancake and roll.
Pop into a warm oven-proof dish and cook for a further 10 minutes.
Serve on a bed of salad and garnish with the prawns and parsley.

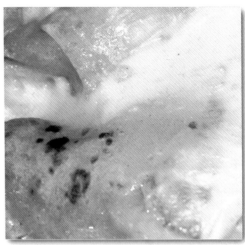

Sassy Cho-Cho and Tiger Prawns

Ingredients

2 cho-cho
8oz peeled tiger prawns
3 spring onions
3 tbsp olive oil
1 tsp salt
½ tsp ground black pepper
3 tbsp basil, chopped
4 fl oz single cream

4 tbsp olive oil
1 tsp Rustie's Hot Pepper Sauce
(see page 22)
2 tsp soy sauce
6 tbsp white wine vinegar
½ tsp salt
1 cos lettuce
½ cucumber
3oz rocket leaves

Method

Approximate cooking time 25 minutes

Peel the cho-cho, cut them in half and scoop out the flat white seed.

In a saucepan of boiling water, add 1 tbsp olive oil and ½ tsp salt and part-boil for 5-8 minutes.

Remove from the heat, pour the water away and allow to cool.

Chop the spring onions and mix together with the basil.

Cut the cho-cho into strips and heat 1 tbsp of olive oil in a heavy-bottomed frying pan.

Add the cho-cho to the pan and sauté for 5 minutes, after which add the spring onion and basil and sauté together for a further 4-5 minutes.

Add the single cream, rest of the salt and a black pepper and allow to simmer for 3-4 minutes.

In a separate frying pan, heat the remaining tablespoon of oil and when smoking, add the peeled tiger prawns.

Stir the mixture altogether and simmer for 2 minutes.

Serve on a bed of salad.

For the salad, put 4 tbsp of olive oil in a bowl and using a whisk, add the pepper sauce, soy sauce and salt.

Whisk altogether, then gradually add the white wine vinegar and continue whisking until emulsified together.

Place the lettuce, cucumber and rocket leaves in the centre of a plate then place the cho-cho and tiger prawns on top.

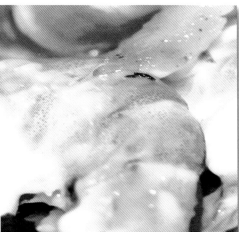

Callaloo With Crab Soup

Ingredients

450g (1lb) callaloo leaves or spinach
225g (8oz) crab meat, flaked
8 crab claws
110g (4oz) salt pork or 6
 rashers bacon, chopped
1 large onion
4 sprigs thyme, chopped
2½ pts chicken stock
2 tsp salt
1 chilli pepper, chopped
2 tbsp vegetable oil

For the Spinners:
110g (4oz) cornmeal
110g (4oz) plain flour
½ tsp salt
Water to bind

Method

Approximate cooking time 40 minutes

Cut the pork or bacon into small pieces and in a Dutchie pot or large saucepan, lightly fry in the oil until they turn golden crispy brown.

Add the callaloo, chopped roughly, together with the onion, chilli pepper, thyme, salt and chicken stock.

Cook for around 20 minutes.

For the spinners, mix the cornmeal, plain flour and salt in a bowl, then bind together with a little water.

Take small pieces of dough and roll between your palms into small sausage shapes, then drop them into the soup mixture.

Allow to cook for approximately 10-12 minutes, then add the flaked crab and claws and cook for a further 4-5 minutes.

Caribbean Fish Soup

Ingredients

450g (1lb) firm white fish
1150g (2pt) fish stock
425g (½pt) white wine
110g (4oz) shrimps
50g (2oz) tomato purée
1 large onion, chopped
1 medium green pepper, chopped
1 large tin chopped tomatoes

4 sprigs basil, chopped
(leaving a few for decoration)
1 tsp white pepper
1 tsp salt
2 dsp plain flour and water for thickening

For the Spinners:
50g (2oz) plain flour
50g (2oz) cornmeal
Water to bind
Pinch of salt

Method

Approximate cooking time 35 minutes

For the spinners, mix the flour and the cornmeal together.

Add the salt and bind the mixture with the water to make a dough.

Take the pieces of dough and roll into small sausage shapes.

For the soup, put the stock in a saucepan and bring to the boil.

Add the onion, pepper, tomatoes and the tomato purée, white pepper, salt and basil allow to cook for 8-10 minutes.

Add the spinners to the stock and cook for approximately 4 minutes.

Chop the fish into chunks and sprinkle with a little salt and pepper.

Add the fish chunks to the stock and cook for 3-4 minutes.

Add the white wine and simmer for 4-5 minutes.

Add the thickener and cook for a further 2-4 minutes, then add the shrimps and cook for 3-4 minutes.

Remove from heat and serve with crusty bread.

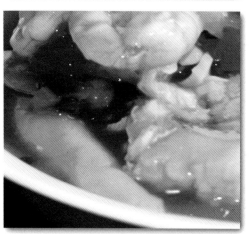

Chunky Pepper Pot Soup

Ingredients

450g (1lb) shin beef
450g (1lb) yam, peeled and chopped into large chunks
225g (8oz) pumpkin
225g (8oz) kidney beans
2 onions, chopped
2 medium tomatoes, chopped
2 tsp salt
2 tsp black pepper
½ scotch bonnet pepper

2 chilli peppers, chopped
1 tbsp fresh thyme
2 cloves garlic
1 beef stock cube
4-4 ½ pts boiling water
115g (4oz) spinach
60g (2oz) coconut cream
6 fl oz vegetable oil

Method

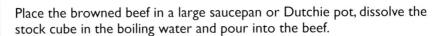

Approximate cooking time 1 hour 30 minutes

Wash and cut the beef into small pieces and season with garlic, salt, black pepper and the chilli pepper.

Fry in hot oil until brown.

Place the browned beef in a large saucepan or Dutchie pot, dissolve the stock cube in the boiling water and pour into the beef.

Add the kidney beans and half of the thyme and cook until meat is tender. (You may need to add more boiling water.)

Chop the onion, tomatoes and scotch bonnet pepper and add to the pot, together with coconut cream and rest of the thyme.

Cook for a further hour, stirring occasionally.

Prepare and make the dumplings (see page 57).

Once the dumplings are made, flatten them and drop them into the soup with the yam and cook for 10 minutes.

Add the pumpkin and spinach and cook for a further 10-15 minutes.

Remove from heat and serve hot.

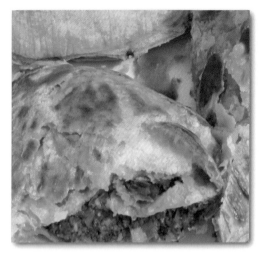

Snacks

I have separated these recipes for you because they are quick and easy to make and would be perfect for lunchbox fillers, party food or if time is of the essence.

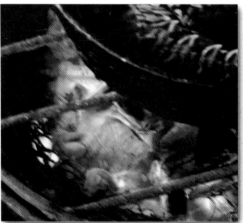

45

Beef Curry Patties

Ingredients

1 block of puff pastry (Approximatly 2lb)
500g minced beef
2 tbsp olive oil
2 cloves garlic, chopped
1 medium onion, chopped
1½ tbsp tomato purée
½ tbsp chilli pepper
3 dsp mild curry powder

6 fl oz water
1 tsp salt
1 tsp black pepper
2 tbsp plain flour
(dissolved in 4 tbsp water to thicken)
2 egg yolks (for the wash)

Method

Approximate cooking time 50 minutes

Add the minced beef to a hot pan and fry for 6-8 minutes.

Drain the fat from the pan and return the meat.

Add the salt, onion and garlic and cook for approximately 10 minutes.

Stir and add the black pepper, curry powder and chilli pepper.

Add the tomato purée and the water, cook for a further 4-5 minutes and stir.

Mix the thickener by dissolving the flour in the water and then add the meat. Cook for a further 2-3 minutes.

Take off the heat and allow to cool.

Roll out the pastry and cut into rounds using a saucer and sharp knife.

Once all the rounds are cut, place approximately 1½ tbsp of mixture in the centre of the pastry.

With the egg wash, brush half the edge of the pastry.

Close the other half over with a fork and press the edges together.

When they are all done in the same way, brush the patties with the egg wash.

Put in a pre-heated oven 180°F and cook for 25-30 minutes until golden.

Chicken Jerk Dough

Ingredients

For the dough:
40g (pkt) yeast
175g (6oz) butter
575 mls (1pt) milk, warmed
3lb strong bread flour
2 tsp sugar
1 tsp salt

For the Filling:
4 x chicken breast
Jerk Seasoning (see page 23)
Oil for cooking

Method

Approximate cooking time with dough, 2 hours

Make up the dough mixture by dissolving the yeast with the sugar in a bowl and add the milk.

Mix the salt with the flour.

Rub in 50g (2oz) of the butter.

Add this mixture to the milk, stir together and mix well.

Knead and allow to stand for 30-40 minutes.

Make the Jerk Chicken according to my recipe on page 120.

Once the Jerk Chicken has been made and the dough has been left to stand for 30-40 minutes, press the dough down firmly and knead again for 2-3 minutes.

Cut the dough into 225g (8oz) pieces and shape each into a ball.

Then with a rolling pin, roll into 'rounds' about 20cm (8in) in diameter.

Place the diced Jerk Chicken in the centre of the dough.

Wet the edges of the dough with cold water, fold the dough in half and press the edges together.

Using your finger, or the handle of a wooden spoon, press holes into the top of the parcel and dot the remaining butter on the top of the dough.

Place on a greased baking tray and allow to rise again in a warm kitchen until doubled in size (approximately 25-30 minutes).

Sprinkle the dough with warm water and bake in a hot oven at 180-200°C for 25-30 minutes.

Serve warm, as a delicious sandwich alternative.

Chicken Pupa-Lickie

Ingredients

6-8 chicken pieces
1 tsp garlic powder or 1 clove garlic
2 tsp paprika
2 tsp salt
1 tsp black pepper
1 tsp thyme
50g (2oz) plain flour
8 fl oz water

For the Batter:
110g (4oz) plain flour
275g (½ pt) milk
1 egg
2 tsp baking powder
1 dsp parsley
2 tsp salt
½ large can sweetcorn
Deep fat or oil for frying

Method

Approximate cooking time 10-20 minutes

Place the paprika, garlic, salt, pepper, thyme and flour in a bowl and mix together.

Coat the chicken pieces with the mixture.

Place the chicken in a pressure cooker with the water and cook for 10 minutes.

Alternatively, if you do not have a pressure cooker you can steam the chicken for 15-20 minutes.

To make the batter, blend the flour, milk, egg, baking powder, parsley and salt.

Beat well until smooth.

Add the sweetcorn and mix well in.

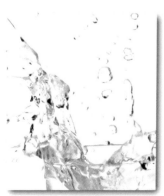

Dip the chicken pieces into the batter, coating well.

Fry in hot oil for 10 minutes.

Drain and serve.

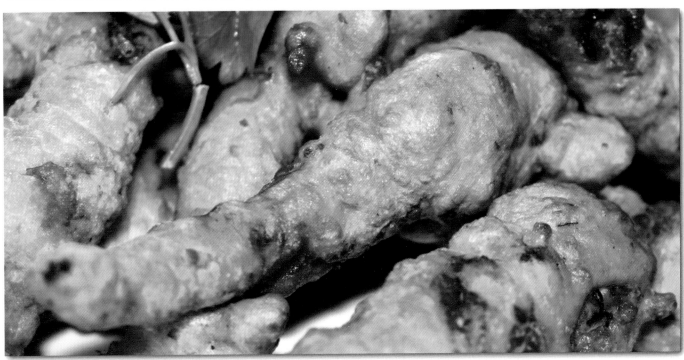

Corn Fritters

Method

Approximate cooking time 5 minutes

Sift the flour together with the baking powder and salt.

Beat the eggs until fluffy.

Add the beaten eggs, sweetcorn, scotch bonnet pepper, melted butter, together with the milk to the dry ingredients.

Use a fork and beat until the mixture has a smooth texture.

The batter should be of a 'dropping' consistency.

Add more milk if desired.

Drop by spoonfuls into preheated deep fat until golden brown.

Ingredients

2 eggs
335g (12oz) flour
6 fl oz milk
2 tsp of baking powder
1 tin sweetcorn, blended
¼ tsp scotch bonnet pepper,
chopped
1 tbsp melted butter
1 tsp salt
Oil for deep frying

Coco Fritters

Method

Approximate cooking time 5 minutes

Peel and grate the coco.

Put the flour, onion, chives, salt and pepper into a deep bowl.

Add the water and beat together.

Fold in the beaten egg white carefully.

Heat the oil and drop spoonfuls of the mixture into it.

Fry until golden.

Drain on kitchen paper, garnish with parsley and serve.

Ingredients

900g (2lb) coco
50g (2oz) plain flour
2 egg-whites, whisked
1 medium onion, grated
6 tbsp water or enough to bind
Few chives, chopped
Salt and pepper to taste
Parsley for garnish
Oil for deep frying

Duckanoo

Method

Approximate cooking time 40-45 minutes

Mix all the ingredients together thoroughly.

Bind with the milk to a 'dropping' consistency.

Place 2 large spoonfuls of the mixture into each foil square.

Fold into parcels and seal the edges.

Steam for 35-40 minutes.

Alternatively, bake in the oven at 190°C for 35-40 minutes.

Ingredients

900g (2lb) cornmeal
225g (8oz) sugar
175g (6oz) butter
175g (6oz) plain flour
1 small coconut, grated
2 tsp vanilla essence
1 tsp salt
2 tsp nutmeg
Milk to mix
8x20 cm (8in) squares of
cooking foil

Sweet Potato Biscuits

Method

Approximate cooking time 30 minutes

In a large bowl put the flour, butter, sweet potato, sugar, coconut, nutmeg, vanilla essence and mix well.

Add a little milk and mix together to the dropping consistency.

Heat the oven to 190°C and place 2 large spoonfuls of the mixture into 4inch pattie tins and bake in the oven for 25-30 minutes.

Ingredients

900g (2 lb) sweet potato grated
225g (8 oz) sugar
175g (6 oz) plain flour
175g (6 oz) butter
1 small coconut, grated
2 tsp nutmeg
2 tsp vanilla essence
1 tsp salt
Milk to mix

Saucy Spare Ribs

Ingredients

900g (2lb) pork ribs
1 large onion, chopped
4 dsp freshly-grated ginger
2 cloves garlic, crushed
3 tbsp clear honey
2 tbsp brown sugar
2 tbsp tomato purée
4 tbsp soy sauce
1 dsp salt
¼ pt vinegar
Cornflour dissolved in water to
thicken

Method

Approximate cooking time 1 hour 40 minutes

Separate the spare ribs and put into a deep, ovenproof dish.

Add all of the other ingredients together and turn them into the meat, coating all over and mixing well.

Cook in a slow oven at 160°C for 1-1½ hours.

After the meat is cooked, remove from the oven and add the cornflour mixture to the meat to thicken the sauce.

Stir altogether and return to the oven.

Cook for a further 10 minutes.

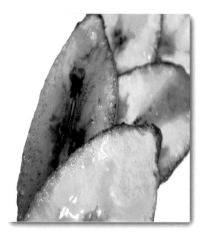

Plantain Crisps
Method

Slice the plantains into reasonable sized rounds or strips.

Dust with the flour and cinnamon.

Heat the oil and fry until golden.

Drain on kitchen paper.

Serve hot or cold with drinks.

Ingredients

2 ripe plantains
2 fl oz olive oil
Flour and cinnamon for dusting

Fried Plantain
Method

Cut the plantains into quarters and skin.

Heat the oil and shallow fry for 6 minutes.

Drain and serve.

Ingredients

2 ripe plantains
Oil for frying

Savoury Dumplings (Spinners)

Method

Approximate cooking time 30 minutes

Rub the butter and flour together in a deep bowl.

Add the baking powder, onion, chives, parsley, salt and pepper, and bind together with enough water to make a stiff dough.

Knead lightly and form into balls.

Heat the oil and deep fry until golden brown.

If you are making spinners to put in casseroles or soups, these will need to be added and cooked for approximately 30 minutes.

Ingredients

110g (4oz) plain flour
3 tbsp butter
1 tsp baking powder
1 tsp onion, chopped
1 tsp chives, chopped
1 tsp parsley, chopped
Pinch of salt and pepper
Water to bind
Oil for deep frying

Journey Cakes

Method

Approximate cooking time 10 minutes

Sieve the flour, salt and baking powder together and rub in the butter.

Add water and make into a dough.

Roll small amounts of the mixture into balls approximatly 2oz and flatten between your palms.

Heat the oil and deep fry or pan fry until golden brown for approximately 6-8 minutes.

Ingredients

450g (1lb) self-raising flour
50g (2oz) butter
1 tsp salt
1 tsp baking powder
150mls (¼ pt) water
Oil for deep frying

Hominy Corn Porridge

Method

Approximate cooking time 35 minutes (in pressure cooker) or 90 minutes (on hob)

Wash the hominy corn.

Place with the salt in a pressure cooker.

Add water and close the pressure cooker and cook for 20-25 minutes until the hominy is soft.

Add the milk, sugar, ¾ of the nutmeg and cook for a further 5 minutes.

Then add the cornflour and cook for a further 2-5 minutes.

If you do not have a pressure cooker, cook the hominy corn for 1-1½ hours on the hob, until soft.

You may need to add more milk or water so the mixture does not dry out.

Sprinkle the rest of the nutmeg over and serve.

Ingredients

280g (10oz) hominy corn
2 pts water
1 pt milk
2 tsp nutmeg
3 dsp cane sugar
2 pinches salt
2 dsp cornflour, dissolved in a little water

Gizadas

Ingredients

For the Filling:
225g (8oz) desiccated coconut
or fresh, finely grated
25g (1oz) butter
110g (4oz) brown sugar
1-2 dsp caramel colouring
2 tsp nutmeg
2 tsp cinnamon
2 tsp vanilla essence
170-225mls (6-8fl oz) water

For the Pastry:
450g (1lb) plain flour
110g (4oz) margarine
50g (2oz) caster sugar
Cold water to bind
(approximatly 4tbs)

Method

Approximate cooking time 25 minutes

To make the pastry, rub the butter and sugar into the flour, bind with the water and allow to stand for 10 minutes.

Roll out on a floured board and with a saucer cut 'rounds' from the pastry.

Pinch up each 'round' into a small pie case.

Place on a greased baking tray.

To make the filling, combine all the ingredients together and mix well.

Fill each pie case with the mixture.

Bake at 180°C for 20-25 minutes.

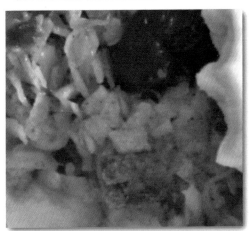

Salad & Vegetables

Whilst in Jamaica, I had the greatest pleasure in visiting some of the amazing markets, which are full of local produce, especially the gungo peas which are famous for being in the traditional recipe "Rice n Peas".

These markets are full of wonderful coloured fruits and vegetables, all of which are traditional in Caribbean cooking. However, let me reassure you that you can buy most of these products in your local supermarket.

I also visited one of the largest fruit plantations in Jamaica – did you know that pineapple bushes only produce one fruit per year? Wow!
Even the lemons grow bigger out there! Though I have to say, my greatest experience was having a coconut picked personally for me from a mature tree by one of the resident farmers.

Next time you visit the supermarket, don't be afraid to pick up something different. We will all recognise the Caribbean vegetable, Irish, as it is our standard potato.

Within the root vegetable family, Caribbean's would favour yams, sweet potatoes and coco.

You may not always be able to buy all the produce fresh, but most, like all other vegetables can be found in tins, such as ackee.

Red Pea & Sweetcorn Salad

Ingredients

225g (8oz) (1 tin) red peas (kidney beans)
450g (1lb) white patna rice, boiled (see page 74)
2 cloves garlic, chopped
Salt and pepper to taste
175g (6oz) sweetcorn, cooked
1 onion, chopped
25g (1oz) fresh ginger, peeled and chopped

For the vinaigrette dressing:
2 tbsp cider vinegar
6-8 tbsp sunflower oil
2 tbsp fresh garden herbs (chives, parsley, basil, etc)
Salt and pepper to season

Method

Approximate cooking time 50 minutes

Drain the kidney beans and heat through with the salt, pepper and garlic.

Cook the rice according to page 74 and mix together with the beans, sweetcorn, ginger and onions in a salad bowl.

To make the dressing, put the herbs, cider vinegar, pepper and oil into a screw-top glass jar, and shake vigorously.

Yam Salad
Method

Approximate preperation and cooking time 30 minutes

Cut the melon into a basket shape and remove the pink flesh (keep it for cocktails later).

Cut the yam into large cubes, mix with the onion, salad cream, salt and pepper and pile into the melon basket.

Decorate with the parsley and strips of avocado.

Ingredients

1 medium watermelon
450g (1lb) yams, boiled for
10-15 minutes and cooled
4 tbsp salad cream
1 small onion, chopped
Salt and pepper to season
2 sprigs of parsley chopped
and half an avocado for
decoration

Sweet Potato Salad
Method

Approximate preperation and cooking time 25 minutes

Peel the sweet potato and boil in salt water for 15-20 minutes.

Drain immediately and dice in a bowl while warm.

Mix with the chopped shallots, butter, pepper, salt and mayonnaise.

Ingredients

450g (1lb) sweet potato
75g (3oz) butter
3 shallots, chopped
Salt and white pepper to season
Mayonnaise to taste

Pumpkin & Cashew Nut Salad

Method

Approximate cooking time 40-45 minutes

Cube the cooked pumpkin and mix together with the other ingredients.

Add the slices of watermelon and green pepper for decoration.

Ingredients

450g (1lb) pumpkin, boiled for
10 minutes and cooled
110g (4oz) cashew nuts
4 tbsp vinaigrette
(oil and vinegar dressing)
Salt and pepper
Slices of watermelon and green
pepper

Coco & Cho-Cho Salad

Method

Approximate preperation and cooking time 25 minutes

Roughly chop the cho-cho and coco and boil.

Once boiled, leave to cool and mix with the other ingredients.

Ingredients

1 medium cho-cho, peeled,
de-seeded and boiled for
10 minutes in salted water
450g (1lb) coco
5 tbsp salad cream
110g (4oz) pistachio nuts,
shelled
Salt and pepper

Ingredients

200mls olive oil
100mls balsamic vinegar
5 tbsp white wine vinegar
2 cloves garlic, crushed
½ tsp salt
½ tsp freshly-ground black
pepper

Vinaigrette

Method

To make the vinaigrette, place all of the ingredients into a glass bottle and shake well, mixing together.

Pour over the salad of your choice.

Store the vinaigrette in an air-tight bottle in the refrigerator.

Rumba Chilli Salad Dressing

Method

Measure the white wine vinegar into a screw top glass jar.

Add all of the other ingredients together and shake vigorously.

Pour mixture over salads or as required.

This is also a very good dressing for fish.

Ingredients

110mls (4fl oz) white wine vinegar
1 tsp dried thyme
1 tsp chilli powder
1 tbsp spring onions, finely chopped
1 tbsp clear, runny honey
1 tbsp white rum
½ tsp salt

Avocado & Chicken Salad with Cream Dressing

Ingredients

3 ripe avocados
225g (8oz) chicken, diced
juice of ½ a lemon
2 tbsp chives, chopped
1 clove garlic, chopped
Salt to season
Paprika for garnish

For the Cream Dressing:
1 small onion, chopped
6 tbsp double cream
2 tsp lemon or lime juice
1 tbsp Dijon mustard
1 tsp parsley, chopped
Salt and pepper to taste

Method

Approximate cooking time 15 minutes

Gently fry the chicken in oil, tossing occasionally.

Peel and stone the avocados.

Cut the avocados into cubes.

Sprinkle with the lemon juice, salt, chives and garlic.

Gently stir in the diced chicken.

To make the cream dressing, mix the onion, salt, pepper, mustard and parsley together.

Bind with the lemon or lime juice, then add the fresh double cream and beat together.

Pour over the salad and garnish with paprika.

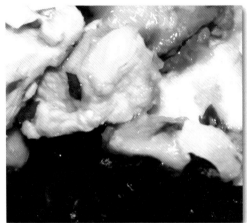

Duck & Yam Salad

Ingredients

½ roast duck, diced (when cooked, ensure that juices run clear)
450g (1lb) yam, peeled, boiled for 10 minutes then diced
110mls (4 fl oz) salad cream
1 tsp cinnamon
1 tsp nutmeg
Salt and pepper to taste
Orange slices, peppers and nuts for decoration

Method

Approximate cooking time 30-40 minutes

Mix all the ingredients together.

Lay out on a serving plate or dish and decorate with the fruit and nuts.

Boiled Rice

This is something I've been saying for years, 'Perfect Rice Every Time', and here's how to achieve it.

Ingredients

450g (1lb) rice
2oz butter
1pt water
1 tsp salt

Method

Put the rice in a saucepan and cover with boiling water.

Boil rapidly for 3-4 minutes.
Strain the water from the rice and rinse through with cold water, drain all the water off.

Then put 2 cups of cold water, the butter and salt into the saucepan.

Cover with a tight lid, return to the hob on a low heat and allow to simmer for 35-40 minutes and stir occasionally.

You will find that the rice grains have all separated.

Like I said, 'Perfect Rice Every Time!'

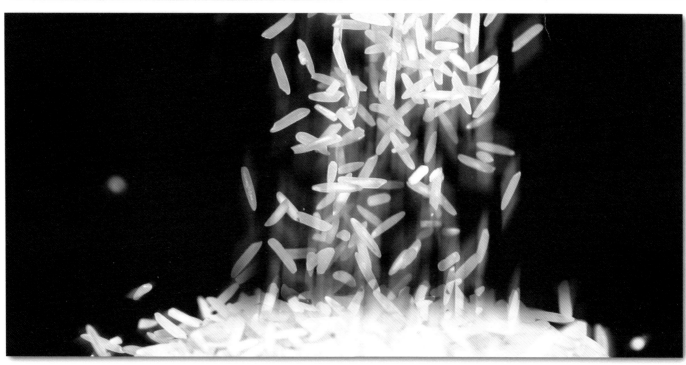

Rice & Gungo Peas

Ingredients

225g (8oz) gungo peas or red kidney beans
450g (1lb) long grain rice (see page 74)
25g (1oz) butter
50g (2oz) coconut cream
½ chilli, de-seeded and chopped
2 tbsp shallots or spring onions, finely chopped
2 tsp thyme, chopped
2-2½ pts water
Salt and black pepper to season

Method

Approximate cooking time 1 hour 30 minutes (cooking time may vary)

Put the gungo peas/red kidney beans into a pan with the thyme, salt, pepper and coconut cream until soft.

(For dried peas and beans cooking times vary, cook untill soft to the touch, you may need to add a cup of water during cooking.)

Add the shallots or spring onions, chilli, butter and rice to the pan and cook for a further 25-30 minutes over a very low heat.

Sweet Potato and Yam Curry

Ingredients

450g (1lb) sweet potatoes (peeled, diced and boiled for 5-6 minutes)
450g (1lb) yam (peeled, diced and boiled for 5-6 minutes)
1 onion
1 pt (1 cube) vegetable stock
2 cloves garlic
4 tsp medium curry powder
1oz ginger

3 tsp thyme
1 dsp coriander
2 dsp plain flour
2 tbsp vegetable oil
1 tsp salt
1 tsp pepper

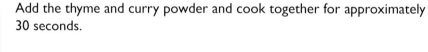

Method

Approximate cooking time 20 minutes

Sauté and sweat off the onion, garlic and ginger in the oil.

Add the thyme and curry powder and cook together for approximately 30 seconds.

Add the stock a bit at a time (keeping some back), together with the salt and pepper.

Dissolve the flour in the remaining stock and pour in while mixing.

Add the coriander, keeping some back for garnish.

Once the sweet potato and yam have boiled, add to the pan, stirring continuously and cook for a further 2-3 minutes.

Garnish with the remaining coriander.

Either serve on its own or on a bed of lettuce.

Stuffed Potatoes

Ingredients

12 medium-sized potatoes
450g (1lb) soya mince or cous cous
2 large onions
2 vegetable stock cubes
425mls (¾ pt) water
4 tbsp tomato purée
1 dsp basil
Salt and pepper to season
Oil for frying

Method

Approximate cooking time 45 minutes

Peel the potatoes and cut across the top.

Scoop out the centre and then deep-fry both the potatoes and centres until light brown.

Remove from heat and drain off the oil.

Fry the onions and dissolve 1 vegetable stock cube in half of the water.

Add the soya mince of cous cous, salt and pepper and cook until the desired texture is achieved.

Add tomato purée and cook for a further 10 minutes.

Continue stirring the mixture and add in the basil.

Place the fried centre parts of the potatoes along with some of the mixture on the bottom of the saucepan and arrange the potatoes upright on top of the mixture, making sure they fit tightly so they do not fall over.

Using a teaspoon, stuff the potatoes with the remaining mixture.

Dissolve the other stock cube in the remaining water and pour over the potatoes.

Cook for 25-30 minutes at 190°C.

Stuffed Peppers, Vegetarian Style

Ingredients

110g (4oz) soya mince or cous cous
450g (1lb) long grain rice, cooked (see page 74)
8 large peppers
25g (1oz) coconut cream
2 medium tomatoes, chopped
2 tsp tomato purée
½ medium onion, chopped
1 tsp rosemary
1 tsp chilli powder
1 tsp thyme
1 ½ pts water
Salt and pepper to season

Method

Approximate cooking time 1 hour

Boil the soya mince, coconut cream, salt and pepper in about 850mls (1½ pts) water for 10-15 minutes.

Drain and keep the juice.

Mix together with the cooked rice, tomatoes, onion, rosemary, chilli powder, thyme and tomato purée.

Cut the tops off the peppers and keep to one side.

Remove the seeds and pith and stuff with the mixture, filling to the top.

Stand the peppers in an ovenproof, high sided dish, pour the drained juice from the soya mince over, replace the tops on the peppers and bake for 35-40 minutes at 160°C.

Add prawns for a fish alternative.

Conkies

Ingredients

175g (6oz) grated coconut
110g (4oz) pumpkin, peeled and grated
225g (8oz) sweet potatoes
175g (6oz) brown sugar
2 tsp allspice
2 tsp nutmeg
2 tsp almond essence

175g (6oz) stoned raisins
75g (3oz) plain flour
225g (8oz) cornmeal
175g (6oz) butter, melted
275mls (½ pt) milk
20cm (8in) squares of cooking foil to make the parcels, as required

Method

Approximate cooking time 30 minutes – 1 hour

In a deep bowl, combine all the ingredients and mix well.

Spread the squares of cooking foil out flat on a table and with a large spoon put 2-3 spoonfuls into the centre of the foil.

Fold over into a parcel shape and seal the edges with the fingers.

Steam in a pressure cooker for 30 minutes or in a steamer over a pan of boiling water for 1 hour.

Fried Yam Cakes

Method

Approximate cooking time 30 minutes

Boil the yams or sweet potatoes for about 25 minutes until tender.

Pour away the water and mash in a deep bowl with the butter.

Add the onions, parsley, salt and pepper and mix in well.

Drop in the egg yolks, one at a time, and beat well until the mixture is fairly smooth.

(Use a food mixer to combine all the ingredients).

Heat the oil in a large heavy pan.

Drop tablespoonfuls of the yam mixture into the oil and cook 4 to 5 at a time, leaving room for them to spread.

Cook for about 5 minutes each side until golden brown and crisp.

Ingredients

675g (1½lb) fresh yams
(or sweet potatoes)
25g (1oz) butter
3 egg yolks
1 small onion, finely grated
4 tbsp vegetable oil
2 tbsp fresh parsley, finely chopped
2 tsp salt
2 tsp black pepper

Crunchy Crushed Yam

Method

Approximate cooking time 45 minutes

Peel, boil or steam the yam for 20-25 minutes.

Mash with a fork in a bowl and add butter, salt and pepper.

Heat the oil in a baking tray and add the yam.

Roast for 15-20 minutes at 180°C.

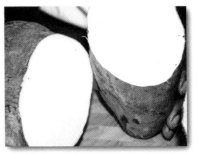

Ingredients

450g (1lb) yam
115g (4oz) butter
1 tsp salt
½ tsp pepper
4 dsp oil

Curried Creamy Okras

Ingredients

450g (1lb) okras
3 cloves garlic
25g (1oz) fresh ginger (root ginger)
50g (2oz) coconut cream
½ tsp salt
5 tbsp olive oil
½ pt vegetable stock
1 tbsp mild curry powder
4 sprigs basil
¼ scotch bonnet pepper
6 spring onions
1 small tin chopped tomatoes

Method

Approximate cooking time 25 minutes

Wash the okras and cut the stalks off and dry them.

Chop the garlic, root ginger, scotch bonnet pepper, spring onion and basil leaving some for decoration.

Heat the Dutchie pot or frying pan and add the olive oil.

Add the salt and chopped vegetables, except for the okras, and the remaining basil in the hot oil and sweat for approximately 2 minutes.

Sprinkle in the curry powder and stir in the chopped tomatoes.

Cook for a further minute.

Add the okras and stir in the vegetable stock.

Lower the heat and simmer for 10 minutes.

Mix in the coconut cream and cook for a further 5-8 minutes.

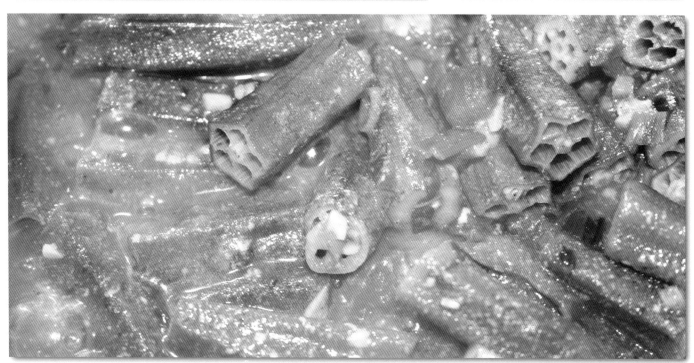

Aubergine (Eggplant) Bake

Ingredients

2 medium aubergines
425g (1 tin) tomatoes
50g (2oz) white breadcrumbs
50g (2oz) grated cheese for topping
3 tbsp butter
3 tbsp plain flour
1 small onion, chopped
1 medium green pepper,
de-seeded and chopped
1 tbsp brown sugar
1 tsp salt
½ bay leaf
2 cloves garlic

Method

Approximate cooking time 45 minutes

Peel the aubergines and cut into small pieces and boil in a small amount of water until tender.

Drain and place in a greased dish.

Melt the butter and add the tomatoes, flour, green pepper, onion, brown sugar, garlic, salt and bay leaf.

Cook for 5 minutes over a medium heat, stirring continuously.

Pour the mixture over the aubergines, sprinkle with the breadcrumbs and grated cheese.

Bake in a moderate oven at 180°C for 30 minutes.

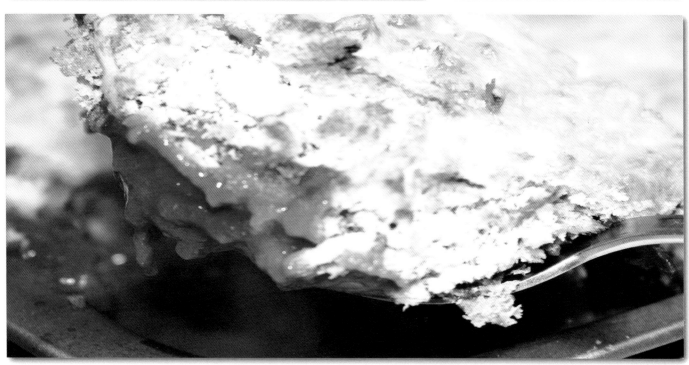

Cornbake

Ingredients

2 eggs
25g (1oz) butter
75g (3oz) cornmeal
1 small can sweetcorn
1 small can evaporated milk
1 medium onion, chopped
½ medium green pepper, de-seeded and chopped
Salt and pepper to season

Method

Approximate cooking time 40 minutes

In a blender, combine all of the ingredients except the pepper.

Liquidize until smooth.

Put into a bowl, add the green pepper and mix well.

Turn into a greased baking dish and bake for 30-40 minutes at 150°C until set.

Fish

My first memory of food was when I was a little girl at the age of four, in Jamaica sat by a stream picking out little transparent shrimps and eating them.
But don't worry, I use cooked fish in all of my recipes and you will find that any local fishmongers or supermarket now stock most of the fish mentioned in my recipes.

For generations, the sea has been the Caribbean livelihood and I had enormous joy in meeting a local fisherman and his family. It's not very often that you get to scale, gut, wash and then cook within minutes of catching your meal.

This is exactly what I mean when mentioning wonderful but simple cooking. Low heat and Gas mark 6 does not come into the equation when your stove consists of coal and wheel rims situated on a beach, under an almond tree.

I arrived at their humble home in order to create a special something for my book, but in reality, what they gave to me was far greater; an insight into how uncomplicated life can really be.

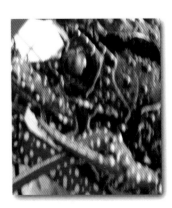

Escoveitch Fish

Ingredients

1.8kg (4lb) whole fish – herring, goatfish, snapper, etc, as preferred
50g (2oz) peppercorns
25g (1oz) pimento seeds
275mls (½pt) vinegar
2 chilli peppers, chopped
½ red pepper, chopped
½ green pepper, chopped
2 onions, chopped
2 cloves garlic, chopped
1 tsp salt
1 tsp white pepper
Oil for frying

Method

Approximate cooking time 20 minutes

Wash and clean the fish and lay flat on a dish, season with a little salt and flat fry for 8 minutes and leave to one side.

Mix together the vinegar, peppercorns, pimento seeds, chilli peppers, red and green peppers, onions, salt and pepper in a saucepan and boil for 8 minutes.

Pour the vinegar mixture over the fish and leave to marinate for at least an hour, then serve cold.

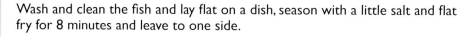

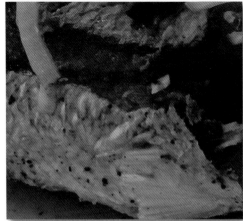

Chunky Caribbean Fish Stew

Ingredients

225g (8oz) tilapia cod or mackerel
335g (12oz) mussels
175g (6oz) shell prawns
280 (10oz) sweet potato
2 medium cho-cho
4 tbsp olive oil
4 bay leaves
6 spring onions
½ pt white wine
2oz coconut cream

2 cloves garlic, chopped
1 whole chilli or ½ tsp chilli flakes
2 carrots, chopped and cooked
3 tomatoes, chopped
1 tbsp basil, chopped
2 tsp salt
1/2 pt boiling water

Method

Approximate cooking time 40 minutes

Steam the sweet potatoes and cho-cho.

After 10 minutes, put aside.

Heat the oil in a hot pan and sweat off the onions, chilli, tomatoes, carrots and garlic.

Slice the fish into strips and add to the mixture.

Cook for 8-10 minutes.

Add the water and stir in the salt and coconut cream until dissolved.

Then pour in the wine.

Add the sweet potatoes, cho-cho and bay leaves and cook for a further 10 minutes.

Add in the mussels and the prawns and cook for a further 3-4 minutes.

Roughly chop the basil and stir in just before you are about to serve.

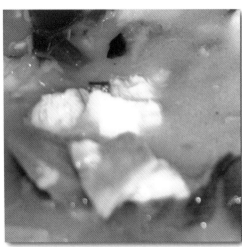
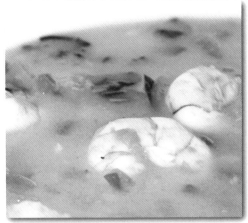

Ackee & Salt Fish

Ingredients

1 lb fresh salt fish or cod
1 can ackee (available at specialty markets)
¼ cup vegetable oil
2 strips of bacon cut into smaller strips
1 large onion, chopped
2 medium tomatoes, chopped
1 medium pepper, chopped
1 tsp salt
1 tsp fresh ground pepper
4 sprigs parsley, chopped
(leave a bit aside for garnish)

Method

Approximate cooking time 40 minutes

Soak the fish overnight to extract the salt; failing this, boil the fish in water for 10 minutes then wash through.

Remove the skin and bones and flake the fish.

Open the tin of ackee, drain of the liquid and set aside.

Heat the oil in a large frying-pan and fry the bacon for approximately 3 minutes.

Add the onions, tomatoes, peppers, parsley and a pinch of salt and cook for 5 minutes, stirring gently.

Add the fish, black pepper and rest of the salt and cook for 5 minutes untill completely heated thorugh.

Then add the ackee and cook for a further 3-4 minutes.

During cooking, turn the mixture over gently as the ackee is very fragile.

Serve this dish with either boiled green bananas or on a bed of rice and garnish with the remaining parsley.

Cod Fish, Pineapple & Rice

Ingredients

225g (8oz) cod fish
(cook in a little milk and butter if braising)
450g (1lb) long grain rice (see page 74)
225g (8oz) prawns cooked and peeled
110mls (4 fl oz) vinaigrette (oil and vinegar dressing)
2 medium pineapples
Red pepper, lettuce and tomato for decoration
Salt and pepper to season

Method

Approximate cooking time 1 hour.

Cook the rice referring to page 74 and remove from the heat.

Grill the cod or braise in a little milk and butter and season with salt and pepper to taste.

Roughly flake the cod and add to the rice with half of the prawns.

Add a little vinaigrette and season again to taste.

Halve the pineapples lengthways, scoop out the flesh and chop it roughly.

Mix with the fish and cooked rice and put back into the pineapple shells.

Decorate with the remaining prawns, strips of red pepper and tomato on a bed of lettuce leaves.

Poached Salmon

Ingredients

3.2kg (7lb) salmon whole steaks
10 peppercorns
2 lemons, roughly chopped
2 medium onions, roughly chopped
2 bay leaves
1 tsp salt
Water

For the Decoration:
225g (8oz) prawns, cooked
1 pkt gelatine
½ cucumber
2 eggs, hardboiled
3-6 olives

Method

Approximate cooking time 25 minutes

Clean the fish and using a poaching pan, or a large flat cooking vessel, lay the salmon in the pan.

Cover with water, add the bay leaves, peppercorns, lemons, onions and salt.

Poach over a low heat for 20-25 minutes.

Remove from the heat and allow to cool.

Prepare the gelatine as per the instructions on the packaging.

Drain the salmon and place in a large flat dish.

Paint the gelatine over the fish.

Slice the cucumber and the eggs and decorate, using the prawns and olives, to your own design.

Mackerel Run Dung (Down)

Ingredients

2lbs pickled, boneless
mackerel
½ pt water
1 tbsp vinegar
4 sprigs thyme
2 garlic cloves, crushed
1 large onion, finely chopped
2 large tomatoes, finely chopped
1 Scotch bonnet pepper
2 stalks spring onion, finely chopped
1pt coconut milk
Salt and black pepper to season

Method

Approximate cooking time 35 minutes

To remove some of the salt from the mackerel, soak in the water overnight or boil for 10 minutes.

Drain the water from the mackerel and cut into pieces.

Combine the coconut milk and water in a frying pan and boil until it looks oily.

Add the mackerel and cover the pan.

Cook for 12 minutes on a medium heat.

Add and stir in the onion, garlic, spring onions, tomatoes, Scotch bonnet pepper, thyme and vinegar.

Add salt and pepper to taste.

Lower the heat and simmer for at least 10 minutes.

Serve with bananas, yam, roast breadfruit or dumplings.

Shark Muhammad

I created this dish in honour of that great champion boxer, Muhammad Ali, when he came to eat at my restaurant in Birmingham.
It was a speciality of the house.
Very rich, it is definitely a dish for a very special occasion.

Not only does shark taste delicious, you have just the one central bone to worry about; the rest is beautiful firm flesh.

Shark Muhammad

Ingredients

900g (2lb) shark, cut into rounds
(if not available, use swordfish)
2 tsp salt
2 tsp pepper
25g (1oz) butter
1 dsp paprika
1 red & 1 green pepper, chopped
¼ courgette, chopped
2 tomatoes, chopped
50g (2oz) mushrooms, chopped

1 onion, chopped
1 avocado
2 tbsp tomato purée
25g (1oz) plain flour
275mls (½pt) sweet white wine
225g (8oz) shrimps
175g (6oz) crabmeat
4 oysters
16 langoustines
Bunch parsley and sweet pepper rings for garnish

For each serving:
Make a bed of stewed callaloo, or cooked greens:
½ onion
1 tomato, chopped
knob of butter
1 tin callaloo, cooked
Salt and pepper to taste

Method

Approximate cooking time 25 minutes

Season the fish to taste with the salt and pepper.

Grill or pan fry on each side for about 5 minutes.

Wrap in foil and keep warm.

In a pan, dissolve the butter and add the paprika, red and green peppers,

courgette, tomatoes, mushrooms and onion and sauté for 4-5 minutes.

Peel the avocado, slice and add the fish to the pan.

Cook for a further 2 minutes.

Add the tomato purée and flour stir gently until cooked.

Keeping back 125mls, add the white wine to the pan and allow to simmer for 3-4 minutes, then add the shrimps and crabmeat and cook for a further 2 minutes.

Grill the oysters under a very low heat for 1-2 minutes.

Pan fry the langoustines for 2-3 minutes on each side with the rest of the white wine.

To make the callaloo, add the salt and pepper and cook for 2-3 minutes.

Sauté the chopped onion and tomato in the butter until soft, but not brown.

To serve, form a bed of callaloo on the plate, place a helping of the mixture from the pan on the callaloo and lay a portion of the fish on top.

Add the white wine to the juices from the pan and pour over the fish.

Place an oyster in the centre; decorate with langoustines, sweet pepper and parsley.

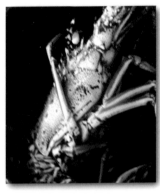

Lobster Sea Breeze

Ingredients

1 large lobster, fresh
(1lb 8 ozs)
1 onion finely chopped
1 tomato, chopped
¼ scotch bonnet pepper,
chopped
½ tsp salt
6fl oz single cream
2 tbsp olive oil
Pinch of black pepper
8 allspice corns
3 sprigs thyme, chopped
leaving some for decoration

Method

Approximate cooking time 25 minutes

Fill a large pot of water and bring to the boil.

Add salt and approximately 8 allspice corns.

Put the lobster in boiling water and allow to cook for 5 minutes.

Remove from the water and allow to cool a little.

With a sharp knife, cut through the head and right down to the tail until you have a complete half.

This will serve two people.

Remove the white flesh and break the lobster's claws, removing the meat.

Place on a plate and cover. Wash the shell out ready to put filling back in.

Pull out the dark parts of the lobster and discard what is not meat.

In a saucepan heat the oil, sauté the onions, then add the tomatoes, and thyme and Scotch bonnet pepper.

Chop the lobster meat into good size chunks and add to the pan.

Cook for approximately 2 minutes then add the single cream and cook for a further 4-5 minutes.

Sprinkle with black pepper.

Put the lobster shells on a serving plate and arrange the meat back into the shell. Garnish with sprigs of thyme.

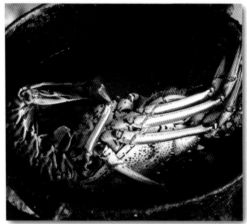

Shabba Delight

Ingredients

1.8kg (4lb) whole fish, as preferred
110g (4oz) okras
2 carrots, chopped
3 shallots, finely chopped
1 red and green pepper, chopped
1 onion
3 sprigs thyme
Juice of 2 limes
Salt and pepper
Oil to bind

Method

Approximate cooking time 20 minutes

Mix the okras, onion, carrots, shallots, pepper, thyme, salt and pepper, and bind with oil.

Slice open, gut and wash the fish, then stuff the mixture into the cavity.

Place in baking foil and squeeze the juice of the limes over the fish.

Then wrap the foil over, creating an envelope.

Bake in the oven for 15-20 minutes at 175°C.

When ready to serve, put onto a plate and pour over the juices and vegetables from the baking foil.

Serve with my favourite dumplings, see page 57.

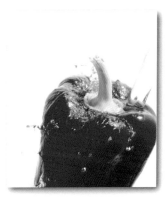

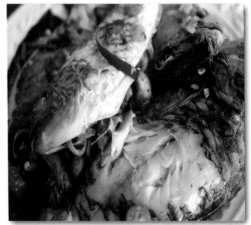

Prawns in Pineapple Port of Spain

Ingredients

350g (12oz) peeled prawns (keep a few for decoration)
Juice of 2 limes
1 tsp salt
2 tbsp olive oil
1 onion, peeled and chopped
3 tbsp chives chopped
2 tomatoes, peeled and chopped
2 tbsp mild curry powder
275ml (1/2 pt) fish stock or water
25g (1oz) plain flour
25g (1oz) butter
1 fresh pineapple or 1 tin of pineapple chunks

Method

Approximate cooking time 40 minutes

Soak the prawns in the limejuice for 20-30 minutes.

Heat the oil and fry the onion together with 2 tsp of chives and tomatoes.

Cook for approximately 2-3 minutes then stir in the curry powder and salt then cook for a further 3-4 minutes.

Gently add the stock continually stirring the mixture, then simmer for 8-10 minutes.

During the time the sauce is simmering, mix together the flour and the butter.

After the 8-10 minutes, start adding the butter and flour in small amounts, stirring continually this will thicken the sauce.

Cook for a further 2-3 minutes.

Cut the pineapple into cubes, and add to the sauce, cook for 2-3 minutes.

Add the prawns to the sauce and heat through for approximately 4-5 minutes more, sprinkle with the remaining chopped chives.

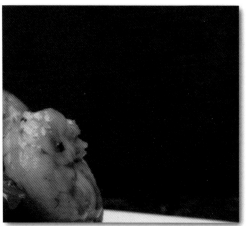

Poultry

I would probably say the most recognized dish in the Caribbean, certainly in Jamaica, would be jerk chicken and there is an amazing recipe for you to try.

I witnessed how great food can be cooked with ease. The huge grills that they were cooking on were racked out with pimento logs, which looked like huge bamboo sticks.
These pimento logs, once heated, bring out the flavours in the food and give it a tender texture.

These were the hottest kitchens I had ever stepped into - it was just like walking into an oven and I was pleased to get out without being cooked myself!

You will see in this next section that cooking isn't all about jerk chicken. I have added in my much-loved recipe, My Favourite Sunday Chicken - try it, I'll bet you'll be adding it to your favourite list too!

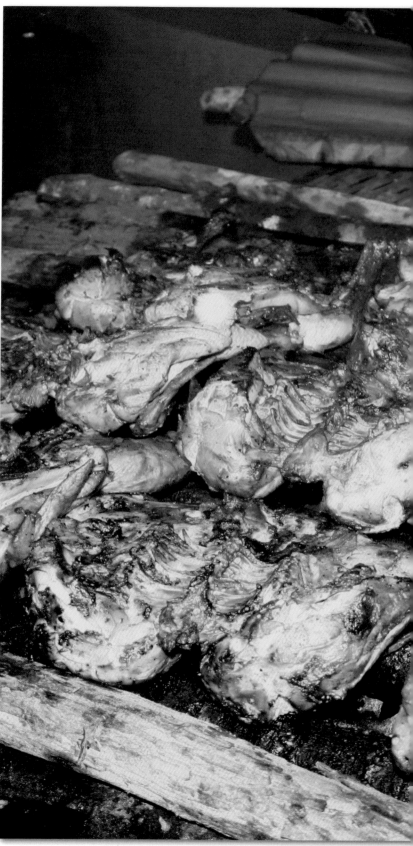

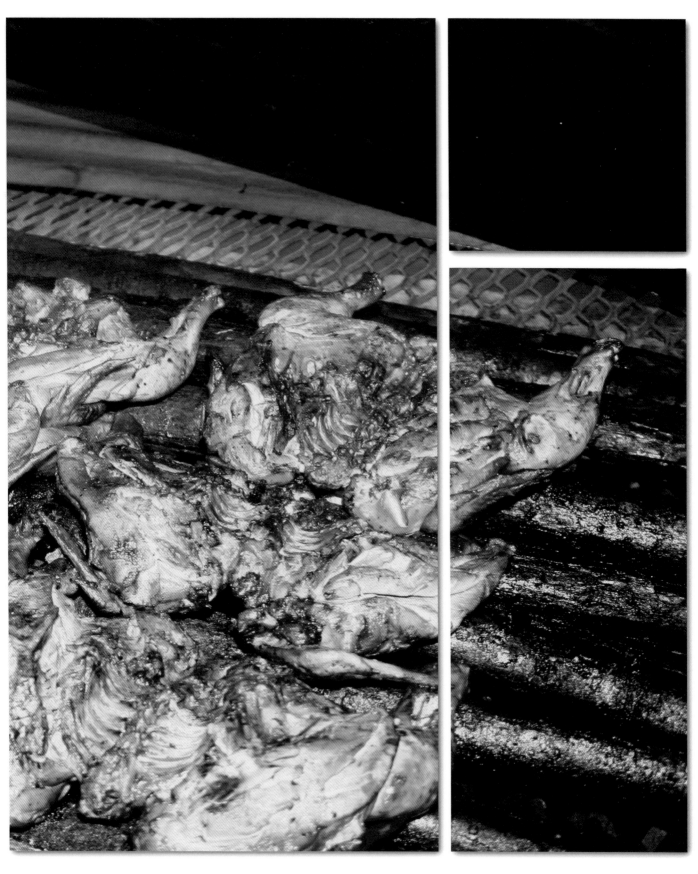

Jerk Chicken

Method

Approximate cooking time 2 hours

Score the chicken and stuff and roll in the jerk seasoning.

Place in a roasting tin, pour over the honey and sprinkle with the brown sugar.

Leave to marinate for at least one hour, but preferably overnight if possible.

If using garlic, push the cloves in decoratively over the surface of the chicken.

Roast for approximately 2 hours at 190°C.

Ingredients

1 whole chicken (4lb) cut into
10-12 pieces
(or chicken breasts)
Jerk seasoning (see page 23)
55ml (2 fl oz) clear honey
55g (2oz) brown sugar
2 garlic cloves (optional)

Jerk Sausage

Method

Approximate cooking time 10 minutes

In a bowl mix together the sausage meat and jerk seasoning.

Flour a chopping board and roll out the mixture into sausage shapes, approximately 55g pieces (2oz).

Place onto a greased tray and grill for 5-7 minutes each side.

Serve with mashed sweet potato or hard dough bread (see page 176).

Ingredients

225g (8oz) good quality pork
sausage meat
85g (3oz) Jerk seasoning
(see page 23)
55g (2oz) flour for binding

Chicken Surprise

Ingredients

350g (12oz) macaroni
3 chicken breasts, boned and skinned
110g (4oz) grated cheese
½ tsp paprika
1 tsp salt
1 tsp black pepper
½ tsp thyme
55mls (2 fl oz) vegetable oil
Parsley for garnish

For the white sauce:
25g (1oz) butter
25g (1oz) plain flour
275ml (½pt) milk

Method

Approximate cooking time 35 minutes

Boil the macaroni for 10 minutes.

Season the chicken with the salt, pepper and thyme.

Fry the chicken in the oil for 6-7 minutes each side.

To make the white sauce, bring the milk to the boil, reduce the heat and add the flour and butter.

Beat until the mixture is of thicker consistency.

Place the macaroni in a dish and put the chicken on the top.

Cover with the white sauce.

Sprinkle with grated cheese and bake in a moderate oven at 180°C for 10-15 minutes, or until golden brown.

Garnish with parsley, sprinkle with paprika and serve with baked potatoes, sweetcorn and peas.

Gingery Chicken

Ingredients

4 chicken breasts
425ml (¾pt) milk
275ml (½pt) coconut milk
2 medium onions, chopped
25g (1 oz) root ginger, peeled and grated
2 tsp chilli powder
2 tsp brown sugar
1 tsp salt
2 cloves garlic, crushed
½ tsp saffron
25g (1 oz) cornflour
4 tbsp olive oil
Grated rind and juice of 2 limes

Method

Approximate cooking time 35 minutes

Wash the chicken breasts, season with the ginger and saffron and mix well.

Squeeze the juice of half a lime over the chicken.

Add the chilli powder, sugar, salt, garlic and onions.

Mix together well and allow to stand.

Heat the pan and add the oil, drop in the chicken, turning occasionally and cook for 6-8 minutes on a moderate heat.

Bring to the boil the milk and coconut milk and add to the chicken.

Cover with a lid and cook for a further 20-25 minutes until tender.

Mix the flour with a little water and stir into the mixture during the last 10 minutes of cooking to thicken.

Chicken Sans Souci

Ingredients

4 chicken pieces
1 large pineapple
1 medium red and 1 medium green pepper,
de-seeded and diced
175g (6oz) brown sugar
175g (6oz) clear thin honey
25g (1oz) cornflour (dissolved in 1 dsp water)
110g (4oz) tomato purée
1 tsp thyme
1 tsp salt
1 tsp black pepper
1 tsp paprika
1 pt (575ml) water
Chopped parsley for garnish

Method

Approximate cooking time 1 hour, 20 minutes

Sprinkle the chicken with salt and pepper, and roast in a pre-heated oven for 15 minutes at 180°C.

Cut the pineapple into four, lengthways.

Remove the core and slice away from the skin and cut into 12 segments.

Mix together in a saucepan the water, sugar, honey, tomato purée, thyme and paprika and bring to the boil.

Dissolve in a small amount of cornflour in the water and add to the boiling mixture.

Add the chicken peices, pineapple and peppers and cook for a further 10-15 minutes.

Spoon the mixture onto the pineapple shells, serve on a bed of long-grain rice and garnish with parsley.

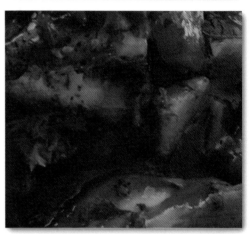

My Sunday Chicken Favourite

Ingredients

1 large chicken cut into approx 8-10 pieces
5 spring onions, chopped
1 large cooking onion, chopped
1 tbsp fresh coriander
1 can chopped tomatoes
110g (4ozs) coconut cream
55mls (2fl oz) soy sauce

2 dsp cajun spice
2 dsp curry powder (see page 23)
2 cloves garlic, chopped
1 green chilli pepper, chopped
110mls (4fl oz) olive oil
1 dsp salt
2 tsp ground black pepper
2 pts chicken stock
Cornflour dissolved in 1 tbsp water

Method

Approximate cooking time 1 hour

Put the chicken in a large bowl, add the cajun spice, curry powder, salt, ground pepper, garlic, onion, spring onion, green chilli pepper and rub into the chicken.

Pour the soy sauce over and stir in. Leave to marinate for at least one hour.

Heat a large Dutchie pot or saucepan until you can feel the heat rising, and then pour in the olive oil.

Place 4 pieces of the chicken in the pot to brown.

This takes roughly 3-5 minutes each side.

Then place them into another bowl.

Repeat the procedure with the other pieces of chicken.

Return all pieces to the Dutchie pot, pour in the stock and cook on a moderate heat, gently stirring occasionally.

Pour in the can of chopped tomatoes, stir and cook for 3-4 minutes.

Cook rapidly for 5 minutes, add the coconut cream and coriander, then turn the heat down and allow to simmer for 30-35 minutes.

After the time allowed, the meat should be tender.

Mix the cornflour and water to make a thickener and pour into the mixture.

Allow to simmer for a further 6-8 minutes.

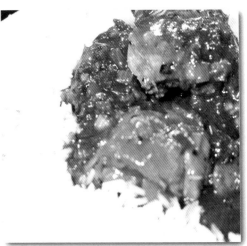

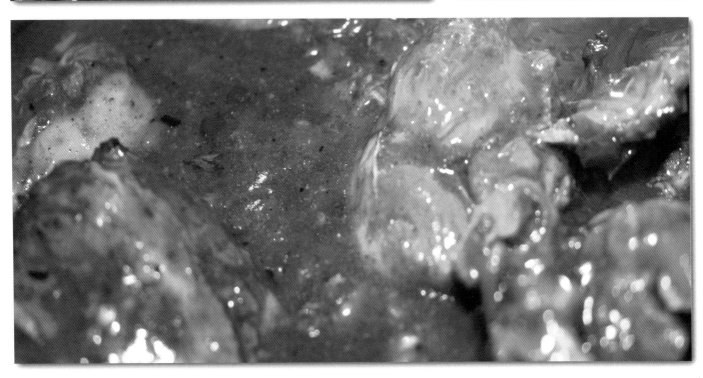

Sweet Pepper Chicken

Method

Approximate cooking time 30 minutes

Cut the red pepper into strips (keeping one strip back for decoration) and sweat down in the heated oil.

Season with salt and pepper.

Mix the tomato purée, chilli powder, curry powder and garlic.

Brush a little oil over the chicken breast and baste in the mixture.

Make 3 slits with a knife on the top of the chicken breasts and place one slice of each coloured pepper into the slits for decoration.

Place on a greased baking tray and cook at 180°c for 20-25 minutes.

Serve with salad or rice.

Ingredients

4 chicken breasts, skinned and boned
2 tbsp tomato purée
1 tsp chilli powder
1 tsp curry powder
2 cloves garlic
1 small red pepper
Salt and pepper
1 slice green pepper
(for decoration)
1 slice yellow pepper
(for decoration)
Oil for frying

Sweet Potato Stuffing for Chicken or Turkey

Method

Approximate cooking time 30 minutes

Heat the oil and fry the sausage meat for approximately 8-10 minutes.

Add the cooked, mashed sweet potatoes together with the breadcrumbs, onions, garlic, nutmeg, thyme, salt and pepper and mix in well.

Allow to cool slightly and roll the mixture into balls with your hands.

Cook for a further 3-5 minutes.

Ingredients

450g (1 lb) sweet potatoes, cooked and mashed
275g (10oz) sausage meat
275g (10oz) soft white breadcrumbs
2 medium onions, chopped
2 tsp grated nutmeg
2 cloves garlic, chopped
3 tsp thyme
2 tbsp vegetable oil
Salt and pepper

Chicken and Rice Stew

Ingredients

1.4kg (3lb) chicken, cut into 8 pieces
225g (8oz) garden peas
2 cloves garlic, chopped
1 large onion
2 dsp freshly ground black pepper
4 tbsp salt
1 red pepper, chopped
1 green pepper, chopped
1 tbsp curry powder

2 tsp cinnamon
2 tsp nutmeg
85ml (3 fl oz) vegetable oil
1 dsp brown sugar
3 pts chicken stock
4 tomatoes, peeled, seeded and chopped
450g (1lb) long-grain white rice (see page 74)
Sliced lemon

Method

Approximate cooking time 1 hour

Skin the chicken and put the pieces in a bowl.

Mix together the garlic, black pepper, salt, curry powder, cinnamon and nutmeg.

Coat the chicken by turning in the mixture.

The chicken can be left overnight so that the spices soak into the chicken. Or leave to marinate for at least one hour.

Pour the oil into a hot pan.

Add the sugar; when it starts to dissolve and to caramelize, fry the pieces of chicken until golden brown.

Once fried, transfer to a container and keep warm.

Cook the rice as shown on page 74 and once cooked add the chicken, and the stock to the rice and cook for approximately 10 minutes on a low heat, stirring occasionally.

Add the peas, chopped peppers, onion and tomatoes to the chicken and rice and cook for a further 30-40 minutes on a low heat.

Garnish with slices of lemon.

Chicken in Pineapple (Portlander)

Ingredients

1½lb (675g) diced chicken breast
575mls (1 pt) chicken stock or water
2 tbspl (1 oz) vegetable oil
1 medium onion
1 red pepper, chopped
2 tbsp mild curry powder
2 medium tomatoes
2 medium pineapples
25g (1oz) plain flour
25g (1oz) butter
2 tsp salt
1 tsp ground black pepper
4 sprigs of coriander, chopped (leaving some for garnish)

Method

Approximate cooking time 40 minutes

Put the chicken pieces in a bowl and season with the salt, pepper and curry powder.

If possible, leave for a few hours to marinate.

Heat the oil in a saucepan and fry the pieces of chicken for approximately 5 minutes.

Pour the stock over the chicken and cook for 3 minutes on a high heat.

Lower the heat and add the onions, peppers, coriander and tomatoes.

Simmer for 18-20 minutes.

Cut each pineapple in half, lengthways.

Cut out the flesh, leaving an empty shell. Dice the flesh.

Rub the flour and butter together and gradually add to the pan.

Stir until smooth.

Add the pineapple pieces and most of the coriander and cook for a further 6 minutes.

When cooked, spoon the chicken, vegetables and chopped pineapple into the pineapple shells.

Garnish with the remaining coriander.

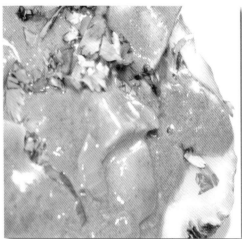

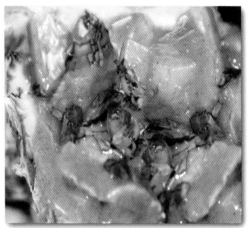

Meats

Of course, the traditional jerk seasoning is still used in meats, so the next time you are cooking sausage and mash, why not try making my jerk sausages as an alternative.

A traditional dish, such as curried goat, which might not sound so delicious, but, I can assure you it is really lovely, is just one of the recipes I urge you to try. I call this recipe Mutton Devil Creek and if goat does not take your fancy, then try it with lamb; either way, it has the most amazing taste.

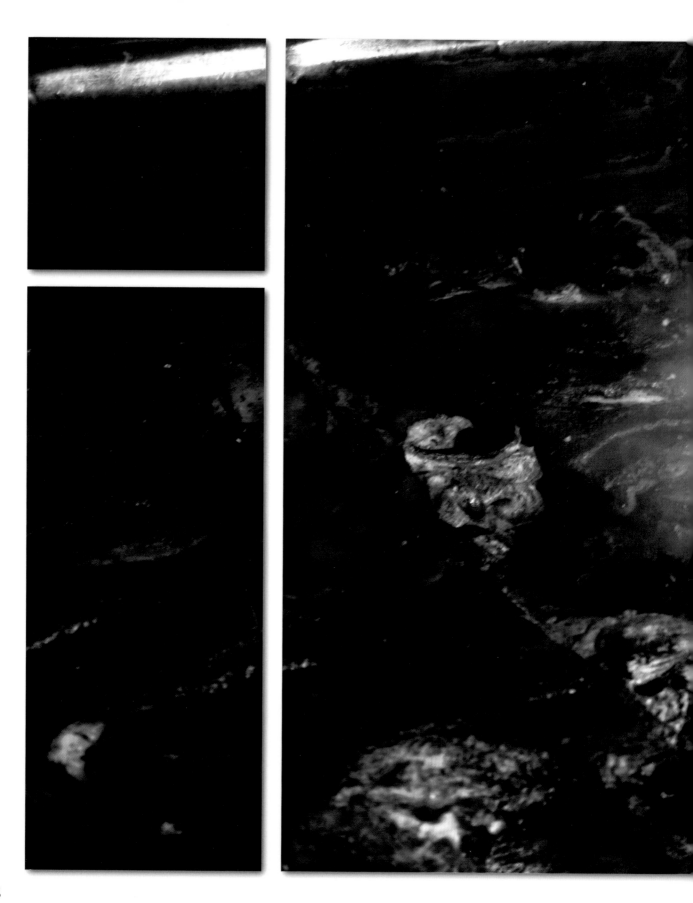

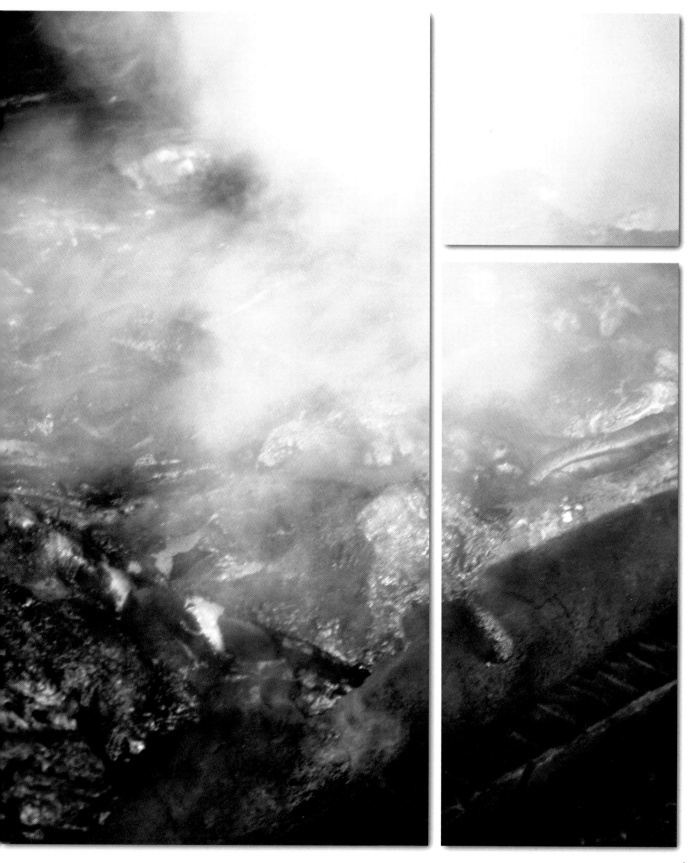

Mutton Devil Creek

Ingredients

900g (2lb) mutton, cut into 5cm (2in) cubes
2 pts lamb stock
4 cloves garlic, finely chopped
2 large onions, chopped
3 carrots, peeled and chopped
I scotch bonnet pepper, chopped
2 sprigs fresh thyme
3 dsp hot curry powder
4 tbsp vegetable oil
2 tbsp plain flour, dissolved in cold water for thickening
I tbsp tomato purée
2 tsp salt
2 tsp ground black pepper

Method

Approximate cooking time I hour 10 minutes

Season the meat with the curry powder, garlic, onions, black pepper, salt and sprigs of thyme.

Leave to marinate overnight, or at least for one hour.

Heat a frying pan and add the oil.

Shake the seasoning off the meat and fry, leaving the seasoning in the bowl.

After you have browned the pieces, scoop them and the juice into a Dutchie Pot (saucepan).

Put the pan on the heat and add the stock and tomato purée and cook on a medium heat for 10-15 minutes.

Then add the scotch bonnet pepper and carrots.

Cook for a further 30-40 minutes, after which, add the thickening mixture and cook for 8-10 minutes on a simmer.

When the meat is tender remove the stalks from the thyme.

Serve on a bed of white rice.

Roast Pork Calypso

Ingredients

2.7kg (6lb) lean pork loin
(preferably the middle cut)
1 pkt (570ml) chicken stock
225g (8oz) brown sugar
28ml (1 fl oz) clear honey
2½ tsp ground ginger, or 25g (1oz)
root ginger, peeled and grated
2 cloves garlic, chopped
2½tsp dark rum
1 bay leaf, crumbled
2 tsp salt
2 tsp black pepper

For the sauce:
3 tbsp light rum
1 dsp cornflour, dissolved with 4
tsp cold water
2½ tsp strained, fresh lemon juice

Method

Approximate cooking time 2 hours 10 minutes

Pre-heat the oven to 180°C. Lightly score the skin of the pork with a sharp knife and place skin side up, in a shallow roasting tin.

Roast at the top of the oven for 1¾ hours, until golden brown.

Remove from the tin and place in a dish.

Skim fat from the pan and add the stock.

In a bowl, mix the sugar, garlic, ginger, dark rum, bay leaf, salt and pepper.

Spread this mixture over the scored side of the pork with a knife.

Place the meat back in the tin, fat side up, and roast for another
25-30 minutes until the top is crunchy and brown.

Transfer to a serving dish.

Sauce:

Warm the light rum in a small pan over a low heat.

Set alight off the heat, with a match, moving the pan to and fro until the flame dies away.

Using the liquid from the roasting tin, bring to a quick boil.

Add the dissolved cornflour to the pan, stirring constantly until thickened.

Remove from the heat and stir in the flamed rum and add the lemon juice.

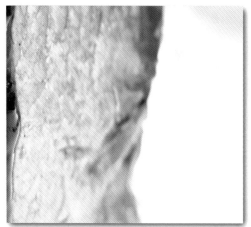
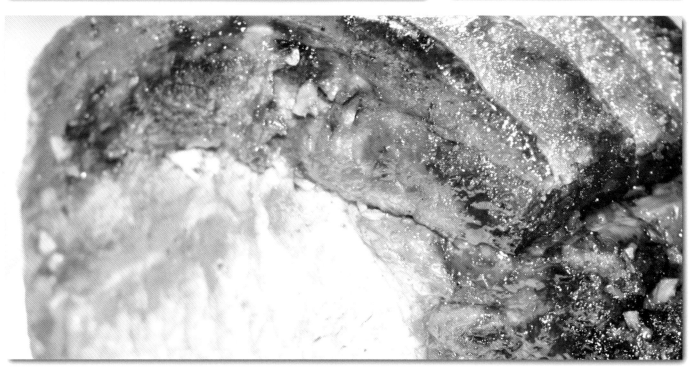

Pork and Cho-Cho in Orange Sauce and Chilli

Ingredients

4 x 6oz (600g) pork chops
1 red bell pepper
2 cloves garlic, chopped
1 tsp flaked chilli peppers
1 whole cho-cho
2 shallots, chopped
4 tbsp olive oil
1 tsp salt
¾ pt fresh orange juice
3 tbsp parsley, finely chopped
3 tbsp honey
3 tbsp soy sauce
2 tbsp cornflour dissolved in 4oz of water

Method

Approximate cooking time 55 minutes

Put the pork chops in a bowl and season with the salt and the flaked chilli, garlic, shallots and parsley.

Allow to stand covered whilst you prepare the bell pepper and cho-cho.

Peel the light green skin away from the cho-cho and cut into chunks.

Wash the pepper, cut in half and remove the stalk and seeds, then slice.

Shake the seasoning off the pork chops and fry each side for 4-5 minutes, then remove from the pan.

Sauté the cho-cho, bell pepper and seasoned shallots and place with the pork chops back into the pan with the orange juice, honey and soy sauce.

Turn the heat down and simmer for 35-40 minutes.
(You may need to add a little more orange juice.)

Stir in the cornflour mixture and cook for a further 4-6 minutes.

Remove from the heat and serve with your favourite vegetables.

Boozy Pork

Ingredients

4 pork chops
1 small onion, chopped
1 medium cooking apple, roughly chopped
2 dsp cornflour
Oil for frying

For the marinade:
2 tsp ginger
1 tsp cinnamon
1 tsp chilli pepper
1 tsp ground pepper
1 can lager

Method

Approximate cooking time 45 minutes

To make the marinade, put the ginger, cinnamon, chilli and pepper in a bowl and mix together.

Coat the chops with this mixture, then add the apple and onion.

Pour over the lager and marinate, ideally overnight, or for at least one hour.

Fry the chops for 5 minutes each side to seal, then cover with a tight-fitting lid and cook over a low heat for 30 minutes.

Mix the cornflour with a little water, add to the pan and cook for a further 10 minutes.

Remove from the heat and serve.

TOWER HAMLETS COLLEGE
POPLAR HIGH STREET
LONDON
E14 0AF

147

Rich Lamb and Sweet Potato Casserole

Ingredients

900g (2lbs) middle neck of lamb cut into joints
450g (1lb) sweet potatoes, peeled and cut into cubes
2 medium onions
2 cloves garlic
1 large can (15oz) chopped tomatoes
2 pts lamb stock
1 level dsp paprika pepper
2 bay leaves
2 tbsp fresh parsley
55mls (2 oz) vegetable oil
Salt and pepper

Method

Approximate cooking time 2 hours

Season the lamb with the paprika, salt and pepper.

Heat the oil and brown the pieces of meat.

Remove after browning and place in a casserole dish.

Fry the onion in the same pan and add the garlic.

Add the tomatoes, bay leaves and meat stock.

Bring to the boil. Pour the mixture over the meat in the casserole dish.

Place in the oven and cook for approximately 1 hour in a moderate oven, 160°C.

Place the potatoes into the casserole and gently stir them through the mixture.

Mix in half of the parsley and cook for a further hour.

Garnish with the remaining parsley.

Lamb Wino

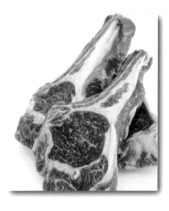

Ingredients

1.4kg (3lb) lamb chops
1 bottle red wine
1 medium onion, chopped
1 tsp paprika
3 bay leaves
1 tbsp parsley, finely chopped
3 cloves garlic, chopped
25g (1oz) plain flour
Water to mix

Method

Approximate cooking time 1 hour

Place the paprika, bay leaves, parsley and garlic into a bowl and mix together.

Coat the chops well.

Add the onion and pour over the bottle of red wine and leave to marinate at room temperature for at least an hour.

Place the marinated chops in an ovenproof dish and cook for 1 hour at 180°C.

Turn the chops over occasionally, at least once during cooking and add more wine if necessary.

Towards the end of the cooking time, thicken the sauce with the flour and water and return to the oven for the rest of the cooking time.

Peppered Steak Caribbean Style

Ingredients

450g (1lb) Sirloin steak
1 tsp salt
1 tsp black pepper
110g (4oz) ground peppercorns
110g French mustard
Oil to fry

For the White Sauce:
25g (1oz) plain flour
275ml (½pt) milk
110mls (4fl.oz) sweet sherry
110mls (4fl.oz) single cream

Method

Approximate cooking time 15 minutes

Beat the steaks flat to tenderize and season with salt and pepper.

Spread the French mustard on both sides of the steaks.

Place the peppercorns on a flat plate.

Dip both sides of the steaks in the ground peppercorns.

Heat the oil and fry the steak for 5-8 minutes each side, or cook to your liking.

Sauce:

Mix the flour and milk together and add to the juice in the pan.

Add the cream and sherry and gently mix in.

Bring to the boil and allow to thicken.

Arrange the steaks on a plate, and pour over the sauce and serve.

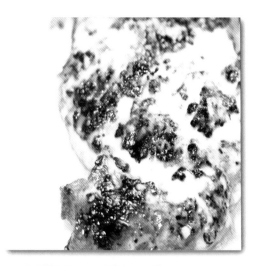
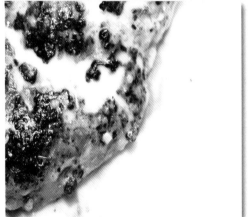

Spicy Beef with Olives & Raisins

Ingredients

1.1kg (2½lb) chuck beef (braising steak)
450g (1 lb) tomatoes, peeled, de-seeded and
finely chopped
75g (3oz) stuffed green olives
50g (2oz) seedless raisins
6 tbsp vegetable oil
1 large onion, finely chopped
2 cloves garlic, finely chopped
2-3 fresh chillies, de-seeded and finely chopped
2 tbsp distilled white vinegar
3 tsp salt
2 tsp pepper
1 tbsp of chopped chives for garnish

Method

Approximate cooking time 2 hours 20 minutes

Trim the excess fat from the meat and cut into 5cm (2in) cubes.

Place in a large, heavy saucepan or a Dutchie pot and season well with the salt and pepper.

Add enough water to cover the meat.

Bring to the boil rapidly and skim the fat off of the water.

Lower the heat, partly cover the pan with a lid and simmer for 1½ - 2 hours until the meat is tender.

In a frying-pan, heat the oil and fry the onion, garlic and chilli for 2-3 minutes and then add to the meat and stir together.

Add the rest of the ingredients and cook for another 5 minutes stirring continuously.

Remove from heat, garnish with the chopped chives and serve.

Corned Beef & Rice

Ingredients

1 can (12oz) corned beef cut into
cubes
1 onion, chopped
½ red pepper, chopped
½ green pepper, chopped
1 can chopped tomatoes
110g (3oz) frozen peas
½ fresh chilli pepper
1 tbsp chopped thyme
4 tbsp olive oil
½ oz butter
½ oz flour
½ pt stock or water
Freshly ground black pepper
Salt

Method

Approximate cooking time 20 minutes

Heat the oil in a large frying pan.

Add the onion and sweat for 2-4 minutes.

Add the red and green peppers and sweat for a further 2 minutes.

Add the chopped tomatoes and chilli pepper and cook for approximately 3 minutes.

Add the peas, cook through again for approximately 3 minutes.

Lightly season with salt and pepper.

Add the stock, allow to start to bubble then mix together the flour and butter and add to thicken the sauce.

Add the thyme.

Add the corned beef and gently turning into the mixture, cook for a further 4-5 minute.

Sprinkle a little thyme on top and serve on a bed of rice.

Spicy Meat Loaf

Ingredients

1½lb minced beef
1½lb minced pork
12 rashes streaky bacon for lining the tin
3 slices bread to make into breadcrumbs
110g (4ozs) medium onions, chopped
2 cloves garlic
110g (4ozs) red and green bell peppers
6 tbsp tomato ketchup

1 tbsp thyme
1 tsp chilli pepper flakes
1 tsp salt
1 tsp black pepper
2 tbsp worcester sauce
1 egg
2 loaf tins

Method

Approximate cooking time 60 mins

In a large bowl, mix together the beef and pork.

Put the bread in a food processor and make into bread crumbs.

Empty the bread crumbs into the meat.

Also in the food processor, place the onions, garlic, peppers and blend until they appear roughly chopped.

Add this into the bowl and mix together well.

Add the egg, tomato ketchup, worcester sauce, chilli flakes, thyme, salt and pepper and mix together well, either by hand or with a spoon.

You will require two loaf tins.

Line one tin with the streaky bacon and place the meat mixture in the two tins.

Cover the top of the tins with baking foil.

Pre-heat the oven to 180°C then place the tins in for 30 minutes.

After, remove from the oven and drain out the oil.

Remove the baking foil and put back into the oven and bake for a further 30 minutes.

When cooled remove from the tin and serve.

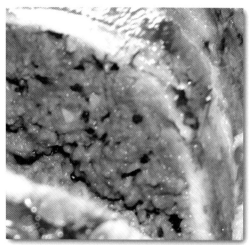

Super Stuffed Beef

Ingredients

1.6kg (3½lb) brisket
2 German sausages or salamis
2 carrots, peeled
Salt and pepper to season
1 large onion
110ml (4fl oz) olive oil
1 bottle red wine
50g (2oz) plain flour

Method

Approximate cooking time 3 hours

Lay meat flat on a board and cut almost through lengthways.

Open out meat and lay the carrots whole along the length of the beef. Season with salt and pepper.

Sweat the onions in the olive oil.

Cut a V shape out of each sausage, and lay them V side down, over the carrots.

Roll meat up into a round and tie well with string.

Place in a deep roasting tin.

Place the onions with the meat and cover with the red wine (keeping a small glass for yourself if your spirits are flagging!).

Slowly roast in the oven for 3 hours at 180°C.

Take out of the oven and leave to stand for a few minutes before carving.

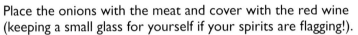

Thicken the sauce in the pan with the flour and pour the sauce over the meat when serving.

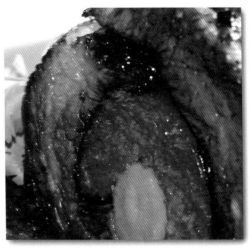

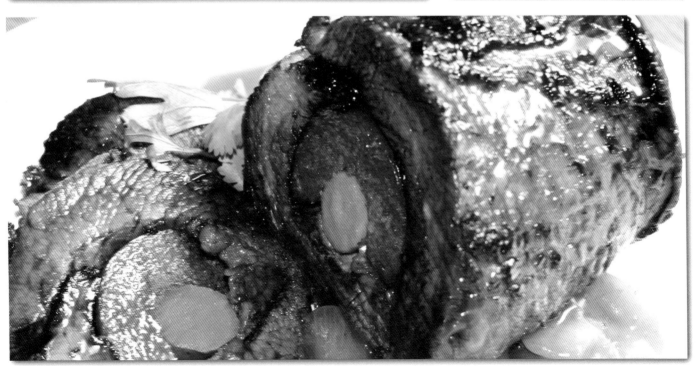

Plantain & Spicy Beef Rings

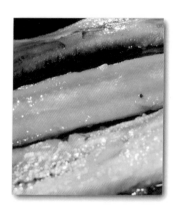

Ingredients

4 ripe plantains
Oil for frying

For the filling:
450g (1lb) lean minced beef
1 small green pepper, finely chopped
1 large tomato, skinned and finely chopped
2 tbsp tomato purée
3fl.oz stock
2 tbsp vegetable oil
2 tsp salt
1 chilli pepper, de-seeded and chopped
110g (4oz) sweetcorn
5 sprigs thyme, keep a little back for garnish

Method

Approximate cooking time 45 minutes

Heat the oil in a heavy pan, add the minced beef, cook for 4-5 minutes continually stirring.

Gradually add the green pepper, tomato, sweetcorn, chilli pepper, salt and thyme.

Continually stirring, add in the tomato purée and gently stir in the stock.

Allow to cook for further 8-10 minutes. Remove from the heat and set aside.

Peel and cut the plantains and slice lengthways.

Pan fry the plantains for approximately 3 minutes each side, then remove from the pan.

Curve each plantain slice round to form a ring and secure with a cocktail stick.

Place the plantain rings on a baking tray.

Spoon the meat and vegetable mixture into the centre of each ring, filling to the top.

Bake in the oven for 15-20 minutes on 190°C.

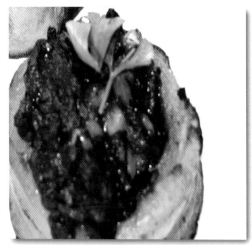

Beef Curry

Ingredients

450g (1lb) shin of beef, cubed
2dsp madras curry powder (hot)
2 tsp salt
2 inch piece of fresh root ginger, chopped
4 bay leaves, crumbled
6 tbsp oil for frying (approximately)
2 cloves garlic, chopped
2 medium onions, chopped
2 tbsp tomato purée
1 beef stock
1 litre boiling water
1 oz flour

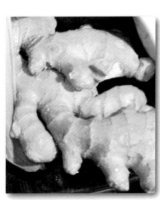

Method

Approximate cooking time 1 hour 15 minutes

Put the flour, salt and curry powder in a bowl and mix well.

This is the coating for the meat.

Place the meat in the mixture and coat until it is completely covered.

Dissolve the beef stock in water.

Pour the oil in a heavy-bottomed frying pan and heat.

Add the meat pieces and brown for approximately 3-4 minutes.

After the meat has browned, transfer to a saucepan and put back on the heat.

Add the water together with the tomato purée, onions, bay leaves, garlic and ginger and stir together.

Turn the heat up and cook for 3-4 minutes, then turn the heat down to a simmer.

Cook the curry for up to 1 hour, until the meat is tender, 15 minutes before the finish cooking time, dissolve the flour in a small amount of water and stir into the mixture.

Return to heat for the last 15 minutes.

Serve on a bed of rice.

Individual Beef Wellington

Ingredients

1.1kg (2½lb) fillet steak (in one piece) slice into
8oz portions
50g (2oz) butter
1 large onion, chopped
225g (8oz) mushrooms, chopped small
2 pkt frozen puff pastry (approximatly 450g 1lb)
110g (4oz) duck pate
1 egg
½ scotch bonnet pepper
(to spice it up, add a whole one)
Mango chutney
2 cloves garlic, chopped
Salt and pepper to taste

Method

Approximate cooking time 50 minutes

Gently fry the steak in the butter to your preference and set aside (covered).

Sweat down the onions, garlic and mushrooms with the scotch bonnet pepper.

Roll the thawed pastry out into an oblong.

Cut into individual 8" squares (or to cover steaks).

Place the cooled seasoned steak in the centre of the pastry and spread the paté over the steak.

Over the paté spread the mango chutney, onion, mushroom and pepper mixture.

Fold over the pastry to make a parcel, brush the edges with water or the beaten egg wash to seal the edges.

With the rest of the remaining beaten egg wash, brush over the top of the pastry parcel and place on a greased baking sheet.

Leave to rest in the fridge for 30 minutes

Make 2 cuts in the pastry and decorate with pastry flowers and leaf shapes (optional).

Bake at 220°C for 35 to 40 minutes, less if you like your meat rare.

Beef Stew

Ingredients

450g (1lb) stewing beef, cubed
225g (8oz) red kidney beans, cooked till soft
900g (2lb) mixed, chopped vegetables
(pumpkin, sweet potato, yam, cho-cho)
50g (2oz) coconut cream
2 cloves garlic, crushed
4 sprigs of thyme, whole
50g (2oz) flour
2 tsp paprika
1 tsp salt
2-3 chillies, chopped
2 large onions, chopped
2 litres stock
Oil for frying

Method

Approximate cooking time 2 hours, 10 minutes

Place the salt, flour and paprika in a mixing bowl and mix together well.

Roll the meat in the mixture until the pieces are completely covered.

Fry the meat in hot oil until browned.

Add the onion and garlic and continue frying. Remove from the pan and place into a saucepan.

Return to the heat and start adding the stock, the kidney beans, sprigs of thyme and chopped chilli peppers.

Cook on a high heat for 8-10 minutes, then lower and simmer for 1 ½ hours.

Keep an eye on the liquid as you might need to add some more stock.

Once simmered, leave to cool for approximately 1 ½ hours.

Then add the coconut cream and stir in.

Add the sweet potatoes and yam and cook for 10 minutes.

Then add the pumpkin and cho-cho and cook for a further 20-30 minutes.

Remove from the heat and serve.

Irish Stew

Ingredients

450g (1lb) stewing lamb
3 large potatoes
2 large carrots
1 large onion
1 tsp salt
1 tsp pepper
1 dsp sugar
½ can Guinness
1150ml (2pt) stock
3 dsp tomato purée
2 tsp parsley
2 tsp thyme
25g (1oz) flour
Oil for frying

Method

Approximate cooking time 1 hour 10 minutes

Heat the oil and put the sugar in the heated oil until it has disolved.

Chop the lamb, season with the salt and pepper.

Add to the hot oil and sugar and fry for approximatly 5 minutes, stirring continuously.

Remove from the frying pan and place into a large saucepan.

Peel the potatoes, onions and carrots and chop them to your own preference.

Add just the carrots and onions to the saucepan with the lamb and stir well.

Pour in the Guinness and the stock and add the potatoes and tomato purée.

Cook for 45 minutes over a low heat, with the lid on.

Mix the flour with a little water and add to the stew with the parsley and thyme.

Stir in well, cover and cook for a further 15 minutes.

Remove from the heat and serve.

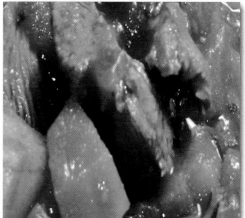

Cakes
&
Breads

Grotto

Method

Approximate baking time 50 minutes, after dough rises

Grease a baking tray.

Mix the yeast and sugar in a bowl.

Pour on the milk, warmed to room temperature, and whisk together.

Sift the flour and salt into a bowl and mix in the butter.

Whisk half the flour mixture into the yeast/milk mixture.

Stand for 30 minutes.

Add the remaining flour mixture to the fermenting yeast/ milk mixture and make into a dough.

Turn out on a floured board and mould for about 5 minutes, until the dough becomes 'elastic'.

(If the dough is sticky, add a little more flour).

Cut the dough into 3 equal pieces.

Mould into 'rounds', and allow to stand in a warm place until doubled in size.

Roll out on a floured board into approximately 20cm (8in) rounds, 2.5cm (1in) thick.

On a floured board, roll out the dough into 2.5cm (1in) thick, 20cm (8in) diameter rounds.

Brush with water, fold in half and then into quarters.

Prick all over with a fork. Place on the baking tray.

Allow to rise in a warm place for 20-25 minutes.

Sprinkle with warm water and bake in a hot oven at 220°C for 25-30 minutes.

Remove from heat, serve either hot or cold.

Ingredients

50g (2oz) fresh yeast
1 tbsp caster sugar
575ml (1 pt) milk
1.4g (3lb) strong bread flour
1 dsp salt
200g (7oz) butter

Coco Bread

Don't expect any cocoa or the vegetable coco, it's just a Jamacian thing...

Method

Approximate cooking time 30 minutes

Dissolve the yeast with the sugar in a bowl and add the milk.
Mix the salt with flour.
Rub in 50g (2oz) of the butter.
Add this mixture to the liquid, stir together and mix well.
Knead and allow to stand for 30-40 minutes.

Press the dough down firmly and knead again for 2-3 minutes.
Cut into 225g (8oz) pieces and shape each into a ball.
Then, with a rolling pin, roll into 'rounds' about 20cm (8in) in diameter.

Dot the top all over with butter. Fold in half. Dot with butter again and fold over.
Using a clean finger, press 'hollows' into the top, and place the bread on a baking tray.
Allow to rise again until doubled in size.
Approximately 25-30 minutes.
Sprinkle with water and bake in a hot oven at 220°C (425°F) Reg 7 for a further 25-30 minutes.

Ingredients

40g (2pkts) yeast
2 tsp sugar
575ml (1 pt) milk, warmed
1 tsp salt
1.4kg (3lb) strong bread flour
175g (6oz) butter

Corn Bread

Method

Approximate cooking time 25 minutes

Sift the flour with the sugar, baking powder and salt; stir in the cornmeal.

Add the eggs, milk and butter. Beat until just smooth.

Pour into a greased loaf pan and bake in a hot oven for 20-25 minutes.

Ingredients

225g (8oz) flour
55g (2oz) sugar
2 tsp baking powder
225g (8oz) yellow cornmeal
2 eggs
¾ tsp salt
½ pt milk
55g (2oz) butter

Hard Dough Bread

Ingredients

1.4kg (3lb) strong bread flour
50g (2oz) dry yeast
50g (2oz) sugar
50g (2ozs) butter
25mls (1fl oz) warm water
8ozs milk (warmed)

Method

Approximate preperation and cooking time 1 hour 50 minutes

Sieve the flour and put into a bowl.

Mix together the yeast, butter, salt, sugar, flour and whisk in the water.

Allow this to stand until it rises.

This will take up to an hour.

Add the dry yeast mixing well together.
Knead into a dough.

Cover the dough with a damp warm cloth and allow to rise again.

This will take another 40-50 minutes depending on the temperature of your kitchen.

When the dough has doubled, it's ready for the next stage.

Cut the dough into 1lb loaves and using a rolling pin, roll out the dough and shape as required.

Allow the loaves to stand until they have risen, again doubling in size.

The loaves can either be baked in a well greased tin or on a well greased oven tray.

Sprinkle with water and place in a pre-heated oven.

Bake for 30-35 minutes on temperature 220°C.

This dough can also be used to make duck bread.

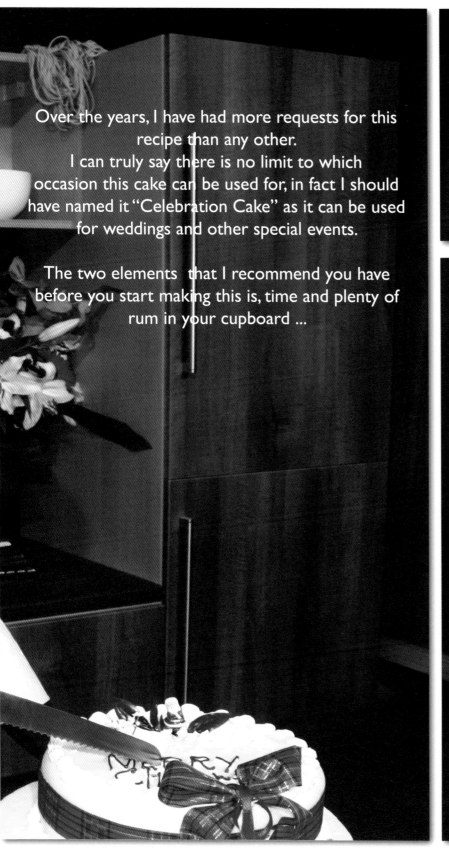

Over the years, I have had more requests for this recipe than any other.
I can truly say there is no limit to which occasion this cake can be used for, in fact I should have named it "Celebration Cake" as it can be used for weddings and other special events.

The two elements that I recommend you have before you start making this is, time and plenty of rum in your cupboard ...

Christmas Cake

Method

Approximate Cooking time 2 hours, 20 minutes; once the mixture has aged for 2 weeks – 2 months

Preparation of this wonderful Christmas Cake takes some time and patience but it is worth it…

Wash and place all the fruit into a large container.

Pour the bottle of ruby wine over the fruit, cover the container with a lid and leave for as long as possible.

This should be for at least two weeks, but for best results leave for up to two months.

If you prefer you could use rum instead of the ruby wine.

I like to use ruby wine because I think it compliments the fruit as it absorbs the wine.

If you haven't got the time to soak the fruit for weeks and months, this is a quick way to get wine into the fruit.

The fruit can be made nice and plump by heating it in a large saucepan with the wine or rum on a medium heat for 4-6 minutes.
Cover the saucepan and simmer for 8-10 minutes stirring occasionally.
Once all the wine is absorbed into the fruit, remove form the heat and allow to cool.

When you are ready to bake your Christmas Cake, cream the butter and the sugar together until the mixture is fluffy; gradually add the eggs and the caramel colouring.

Mix the ground almond, cinnamon and nutmeg into the flour.
Add the dry ingredients to the creamed butter and fold in gently.

Put all the fruit into the cake batter adding the vanilla essence and rum flavouring, mixing together.
Place into two well-lined cake tins, 1 x 10" cake tin containing 6lbs of cake mixture and 1 x 8" cake tin containing approximately 4lb of cake mixture.

Bake at 180°C for 25 minutes and then lower the heat to 150°C for approximately 1hr 40 minutes.
Test the cake with a skewer to make sure it is baked (it will come out dry when done).
Allow the cake to cool for 15 minutes then pour approximately two cups of rum over each cake, and cover.

Allow to stand for a week adding a small amount of rum each day until the entire bottle has been used.

Wrap the cakes up very well with greaseproof paper until you are ready to marzipan.

Coat the cakes with marzipan and allow to stand for two days so that the marzipan sets.

You can then ice and decorate your cake to your own taste and design.

Ingredients

450g (1lbs) pain flour
900g (2lbs) mixed fruit
450g (1lb) sultanas
450g (1lb) butter
450g (1lb) soft brown muscovade sugar
225g (8oz) stoned raisins
225g (8oz) currants
110g (4oz) ground almond
10 eggs
1 tbsp caramel colour
1 dsp cinnamon
1 dsp vanilla essence
1 dsp rum flavour
1 dsp nutmeg
1 bottle ruby wine
1 bottle rum

Banana Cake

Ingredients

5 large ripe bananas
450g (1lb) self-raising flour
175g (6oz) butter
225g (8oz) caster sugar
2 eggs
2 tsp baking powder
Chopped nuts (optional)

Method

Approximate cooking time 40 minutes

Cream the butter and sugar together until fluffy.

Add the eggs, one at a time, whisking continuously.

Mash four bananas and beat into the mixture.

Sieve the flour and baking powder together and fold into the mixture.
Add nuts, if desired.

Grease a loaf tin and put in the mixture. Slice the remaining banana and lay along the top of the cake mix.

Bake for 40 minutes at 180°C or until firm.

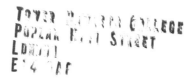

Coconut Cake

Method

Approximate cooking time 55 minutes

Grease and line a 25cm (10in) baking tin. Crack the coconut and husk out the flesh and grate finely.

Cream the butter and sugar together until light and fluffy, then gradually add the eggs.

Then add the flour, baking powder, grated or desiccated coconut and vanilla essence.

Mix together well.

Add the milk gradually until a 'runny' consistency is achieved. Stir in sultanas and pour into the greased and lined baking tin and bake at 160°C for 50-55 minutes.

Ingredients

1 large fresh coconut or 450g (1lb) desiccated coconut.
450g (1lb) self-raising flour
225g (8oz) butter
225g (8oz) soft brown sugar
425ml (¾pt) milk
2 eggs
110g (4oz) sultanas
2 tsp baking powder
1 dsp vanilla essence

Spiced Mango & Nut Ring

Method

Approximate cooking time 50 minutes

Cream together the butter and sugar until light and fluffy.
Gradually add the beaten eggs and beat for approximately 3-4 minutes.

Sieve together the flour and the nutmeg and gently fold into the creamed mixture.

Stir in the chopped mangoes, half of the flaked almonds and the juice of the mango or milk.

Mix until a soft dropping consistency is achieved.

Grease a 25cm (10inch) oven proof ring mould.

Sprinkle the rest of the flaked almonds around the base of the mould and spoon the cake mixture on top of the nuts.

With the back of a spoon, smooth the mixture down around the mould.

Bake the cake for approximately 25 minutes, 180°C, then lower the heat to 150°C and bake the cake for a further 25 minutes.

Test with a skewer or a long sharp knife by pushing into the centre of the cake, if it comes out clean it is cooked.

Allow to cool and turn out onto a plate.

Ingredients

3 mangoes, peeled and chopped
200g (8oz) soft butter
175g (7oz) caster sugar
4 large eggs beaten
8oz (200g) self raising flour
1 tsp nutmeg
110g (4 oz) flaked almonds
3tbs milk or mango juice

Ginger Cake

Method

Approximate cooking time 1 hour 10 minutes

Cream together the butter and sugar and add the eggs gradually.

Then add the golden syrup and mix for 2 minutes, scraping down the sides.

Sieve together the flour, salt, cinnamon and baking powder and add to the mixture.

Stir in both the chopped ginger and crystallized ginger (saving a slice for decoration).

Add the milk and mix to a 'dropping' consistency.

Line a baking tin with grease proof paper and pour in the mixture.

Place in the oven and bake at 180°C for 10 minutes.

Then reduce the temperature to 160°C and bake for a further 40-45 minutes.

Allow the ginger cake to cool for 10-15 minutes.

Mix together the warm water and golden syrup and pour it over the ginger cake.

This will make the cake wonderfully moist.

Ingredients

225 (8oz) self-raising flour
175g (6oz) butter
110g (4oz) soft brown sugar
3 eggs beaten
110ml (4fl oz) golden syrup
50g (1 oz) root ginger, peeled and grated or 2 tsp ground ginger
1 tsp salt
100g (4oz) chooped crystallized ginger
1 tsp cinnamon
1 tsp baking powder
25mls (1 fl oz) milk

Ginger Bickies

Method

Approximate cooking time 10 minutes

Cream the butter and the sugar together for approximately 4 minutes.

Mix together the flour, cocoa powder, cinnamon, bicarbonate of soda, grated root ginger and salt.

Pour the golden syrup into the butter and sugar mixture.

Add the flour mixture and with a wooden spoon mix together.

Then sprinkle the crystallised ginger and continue mixing.

Mould the mixture together, using your hands, into a sausage like roll. Cover with a cloth and stand for 5 minutes.

With a knife, cut disc shapes, approximately 55g (2ozs) each.

Flatten the pieces out on a floured board.

They should be approximately 2 inches across, or you can use a biscuit cutter.

Lightly grease a baking tray and lay the biscuits onto the tray, leaving a little space between each one. Leave for approx. 5 minutes before baking.

Bake at 180°C for 8-10 minutes.
Remove from the oven and allow the biscuits to cool.

Ingredients

225g (8oz) plain flour
75g (3oz) butter
112g (4oz) demerara sugar
25g (1oz) crystallised ginger, chopped
25g (1oz) root ginger, grated
85mls (3fl oz) golden syrup
2tsp bicarbonate soda
1 tbsp cocoa powder
1 tsp cinnamon
Pinch salt

Coconut Drops

Method

Approximate Cooking time 20 minutes

Slice and chop the coconut into small squares and put aside.

In a heavy-bottomed pan, add the sugar and the chopped pieces of coconut together with the caramel colouring, stir together and add the water.

Boil and continue to stir until the temperature reaches 120°C using a sugar thermometer, this temperature is called 'firm ball'.

Remove from the heat and allow to cool for approximately 3-4 minutes.

With a metal spoon, take spoonfuls of the mixture and drop it into the cake cases.

Leave to set for approximatly 1 hour.

Parents and children alike will love these!

Ingredients

225g (8oz) fresh coconut
225g (8oz) granulated sugar
55g (2oz) chopped ginger
¼ tsp caramel colouring
¼ pt water
Cake cases

Spiced Bun

Method

Approximate cooking time 1 hour 5 minutes

Break the egg into a bowl. Mash down the yeast, add the sugar and mix in with your fingers or a spoon. It will become runny.

Add the milk and water, half the flour, the salt and the caramel colouring. Mix well and set aside for 30 minutes.

After this time, add the rest of the flour, the spices and the butter.

Mix well and add the fruit.

Placing the mixture on a floured board, knead well for 5 minutes.

Shape into buns (large or small).

Place on a greased baking sheet. Sprinkle with a little warm water, and allow to rise for 12-15 minutes.

Bake in a pre-heated oven at 220°C for 35 minutes.

For the glaze, mix the sugar and water into a saucepan and bring to the boil, stirring all the time.

Cook for a further 10-15 minutes, allow to cool. (This will be your glaze.)

Once the buns are cooked, brush the glaze over the buns as a finishing touch.

Ingredients

1 egg
50g (2oz) yeast
175g (6oz) soft brown sugar
575ml (1 pt) milk
1.4 kg (3lb) strong bread flour
1 tsp salt
2 tsp caramel colouring
2 tsp nutmeg
2 tsp mixed spice
2 tsp cinnamon
50g (2oz) butter
450g (1 lb) mixed fruit
110g (4oz) glace cherries
275ml (½pt) water

For the Glaze:
110g (4oz) soft brown sugar
275ml (½pt) water

Jamaica Pumpkin Pie

Ingredients

175g (6oz) short-crust pastry
450g (1lb) pumpkin, steamed or stewed
225g (8oz) sugar
1 tsp cinnamon
½ tsp salt
½ tsp ginger
½ tsp allspice
2 eggs, beaten

Method

Approximate cooking time 1 hour

Roll out the pastry and line a 20cm (8in) sponge tin.

Pierce all over the base with a fork.

Mix the pumpkin, sugar, salt, ginger, cinnamon and allspice together in a bowl.

Add the beaten eggs and beat together with your pumpkin mixture for 2 minutes.

Pour into the pastry case and place in a pre-heated oven at 200°C.

Reduce the heat to 180°C after 15 minutes.

Continue to bake for 35-40 minutes and remove from the oven when the pastry is golden brown and the pumpkin custard has set.

Serve hot or cold.

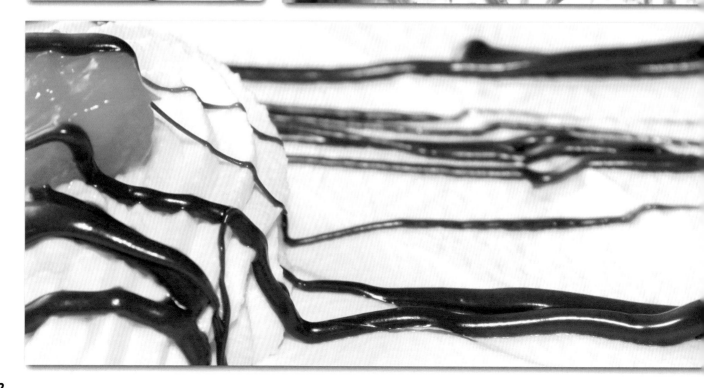

Desserts

Christmas Pudding

Ingredients

225g (8oz) beef suet, chopped
225g (8oz) stoned raisins
225g (8oz) sultanas
350g (12oz) currants
225g (8oz) mixed peel, chopped
225g (8oz) soft brown sugar
225g (8oz) breadcrumbs
75g (3oz) strong flour
20g (¾oz) mixed spice
1 tsp salt
5 eggs
Zest and juice of 2 lemons
Zest and juice of 1 orange
Sherry and rum to taste

Method

Approximate cooking time 4 – 6 hours

In a deep bowl, mix all the ingredients together and allow to stand for 48 hours.

Fill a buttered basin to the brim with the mixture.

Cover with buttered greaseproof paper and tie down with a piece of muslin.

Steam for 4-6 hours, accordingly to the size of the bowl you are using.

To serve, un-mould on a round dish and decorate with a sprig of berried holly.

Pour over some warming spirit (brandy or rum) and light just before bringing to the table.

Mango & Guava Crumble

Method

Approximate prep and cook time 50 minutes

Place the water, guava, mango and approximately 55g (2oz) of the sugar into a saucepan and cook for 5 minutes.

Allow to cool.

Cut the butter into small pieces and place in a large bowl, then add the flour.

Add the nutmeg and remaining sugar to the bowl, with the tips of your fingers, rub together the mixture, it should look like breadcrumbs.

Pour the mangoes and guavas into a over-proof dish and sprinkle the crumble on top.

Put into a pre-heated oven and bake at 180°C for 35-40 minutes until golden.

Ingredients

2 mangoes, peeled and sliced
2 guavas, peeled and sliced
225g (8oz) granulated sugar
225g (8oz) flour
110g (4oz) butter
125mls (5 fl oz) water
1 tsp nutmeg

Pineapple & Mango Pie

Method

Approximate cooking time 40 minutes

To make the pastry, sieve the flour into a deep bowl.

Mix together the butter and sugar into a creamy consistency and add to the flour.

Gradually add in the eggs and knead into a dough.

Take half the pastry out, roll and line a flan dish put in the refrigerator for 15 minutes.

Remove from the refrigerator and bake the pastry base (cover with greaseproof paper in the centre and place heavy beans on top to prevent the pastry rising) for 10 minutes at 190°C (375°F) Reg 5.

Remove from the oven.

To make the filling, peel and core the pineapple and dice saving the top greenery for the decoration.

Slice the mango away from the seed and chop roughly.

In a saucepan put the water, pineapple, mango, sugar, cinnamon and vanilla essence and cook for 3 minutes.

Dissolve the cornflour in a little water and add to this mixture and cook for a further 3 minutes.

Put the mixture into the flan case and roll out the rest of the pastry to make a lid.

Wet the edges with a little water and cover the flan with your pastry lid.

Cut slits in the lid and bake for 20-25 minutes at 190°C.

Allow to cool.

Decorate with the pineapple top by cutting a hole in the centre of the pie and placing the pineapple top into it.

Ingredients

Pastry:
450g (1lb) plain flour
225g (8oz) butter
110g (4oz) caster sugar
2 eggs

Filling:
1 large fresh pineapple
1 large mango, peeled and sliced
110g (4oz) caster sugar
1 tsp cinnamon
1 tsp vanilla essence
275 mls (½pt) water
1 ½ dsp cornflour
50g (2oz) icing sugar

Layered Cake, Caribbean Style

Method

Approximate cooking time 30 minutes

Beat together the butter and sugar until pale and creamy.

Gradually add the beaten eggs mixing in well.

Add the salt to the flour and fold carefully into the mixture.

Add the milk as required to give a soft dropping consistency.

Separate the mixture into two bowls, two-thirds in one and one-third in the other.

To the larger amount, add the pink colouring and the cherries and add the almonds to the smaller quantity.

Divide the large amount between two 20cm (8in) greased and base-lined sandwich tins.

Put the remaining quantity into another prepared tin.

Bake all three at 180°C for 30 minutes.

Sandwich the cakes together with whipped double cream and the jam.

Dust the top with icing sugar before serving.

Ingredients

450g (1 lb) self-raising flour
275ml (½ pt) milk
275ml (½ pt) double cream (whipped)
225g (8oz) butter
225g (8oz) caster sugar
4 medium sized eggs, beaten
75g (3oz) glace cherries, washed and chopped
75g (3oz) chopped almonds
Jar of cherry or guava jam
½ tsp pink colouring
Pinch of salt
Icing sugar to dust

Chocolate Rum & Cake Pots

Method

Approximate preparation time 2 ½ - 3 hours

Break the chocolate into small pieces and put in a bowl.

Place the bowl in a container of boiling water.

Allow the chocolate to melt.

Whisk the egg yolks with the icing sugar and fold the rum and double cream together.

Whisk the egg whites until they are a standing soft peak.

Gently fold the whites into the mixture until all the mixture is combined.

Put one slice of swiss roll in the bottom of six glasses and sprinkle with one desert spoon of rum.

Pour the mixture over the cake.

When they are all filled, put the glasses in the fridge for 2-2½ hours to chill.

Ingredients

250g (9oz) milk chocolate
(keep approximately 25g (1oz)
for decoration)
55g (2 oz) icing sugar
5 tbsp double cream
200mls (8fl oz) fresh double
cream, whisked for decoration
5 eggs, separated
6 slices of swiss roll
4 tbsp dark rum for the pots
6 dsp dark rum to soak the
cake

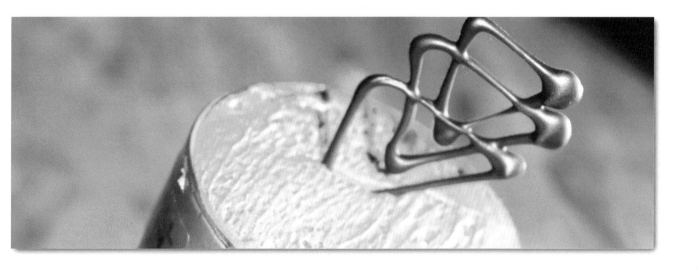

Tipsy Cake

Method

Approximate preparation time 15 minutes

Place the sponge cake or flan base on a large serving plate.

Sprinkle your desired spirit over this and allow to soak in.

Add the nuts to the whipped cream, saving some for decoration.

Spread the cream over the base or sponge cake.

Decorate with nuts and fruit according taste.

Ingredients

1 large sponge cake or
bought flan case
225ml (8fl oz) rum,
Tia Maria or Malibu
575ml (1 pt) whipped cream
110g (4oz) toasted almonds,
flaked glace cherries,
mangoes or strawberries

Banana Fritters

Method

Approximate cooking time 8-10 minutes

Sift the flour into a deep bowl, add the salt and beat in the milk, a little at a time to make a smooth batter.

Set aside for 20-30 minutes.

Whisk the egg whites until stiff and fold into the batter.

Peel the bananas, cut in half lengthways and then into 2 or 3 pieces across.

Coat each piece of banana with the batter and fry in hot oil until golden brown.

Drain on kitchen paper, sprinkle with sugar and serve very hot.

Ingredients

50g (2oz) plain flour
Pinch of salt
2 egg whites
4 tbsp milk
2-3 large bananas
Oil for frying

Alternative

Method

Sift the flour into a deep bowl.

Make a well in the centre and add the egg.

Beat gently into the flour, add the milk, a little at a time to make a smooth batter.

Add the mashed bananas, sugar and spices.

Beat in and leave to rest for 10 minutes in the refrigerator.

Heat the oil in a pan and drop in spoonfuls of the mixture and fry for about 6-8 minutes on each side.

Ingredients

225g (8oz) self-raising flour
1 egg
275ml (½pt) milk
5-6 large ripe bananas, mashed
110g (4oz) sugar
1 tsp nutmeg
1 tsp vanilla essence
Oil for frying

Beauty Cake

Ingredients

275g (10oz) sugar
4 eggs whites
3 tbsp cocoa powder
1 tsp rum essence
2 pkts boudoir biscuits
575msl (1pt) whipping cream, whipped to a stiff peak
1 sachet approximatly 2oz
or 2 leaves of gelatine, approximatly 8inches in size
3 tsp instant coffee powder
Strawberries, guava, raspberries and a
sprig of mint for decoration and any other fruit you desire
1 x 9inch cake ring

Method

Approximate preparation time 30 mins

Whisk together the egg whites and sugar until they reach a stiff peak.

Gradually add in the whipped cream and fold in with the whisked egg whites.

Dissolve the coffee and cocoa powder in a dessert spoon of warm water and add to the mixture with the rum essence and continue to stir in well.

Disolve the gelatine in water acording to its recommended guidlines, when warm stir into the mixture.

Place the ring on the plate you wish to serve your cake on and spread a little of the mixture in the bottom of the ring.

Arange the sponge finger biscuits upright with the bottoms in the mixture round the inside edges of the deep ring.

Make sure the sugar side faces the ring.

Spoon the remaning mixture into the centre of the ring, then fit a plate on the top of the tin to weigh it down.

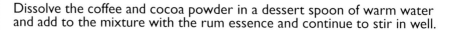

Chill the mixture in the refrigerator overnight.

Once the mixture has set, remove the plate and gently slide the ring off.

To decorate the cake, slice strawberries in half and place upright round the edge of the cake to form a crown.

Then slice the guava and place in a ring inside the strawberries. When you get to the centre of the cake, place a few raspberries and a sprig of mint to complete the decoration or the fruits of your choice.

Rum Truffles

Method

Approximate preparation time 15 minutes

In a bowl crumble the fruit cake, pouring the rum over the cake, mix together.

Roll into balls of approximatly 25g (1oz) to make your truffles.

Break the chocolate into peices and put into a glass bowl over a pot of boiling water slightly smaller that your glass bowl, this will melt your chocolate.

Place your vermicelli chocolate sprinkles into a seperate bowl.

Coat the truffles in the melted chocolate making sure they are fully covered.

Now roll them in the chocolate vermicelli and place into the mini cases.

Leave to set and store in a cool dry place.

Ingredients

225g (8oz) rich fruit cake
175g (6oz) milk/dark chocolate
3 tbsp strong rum
110g (4 oz) chocolate vermicelli
Mini cake cases

Rum Fudge

Method

Approximate cooking time 10 minutes

Dissolve the sugar in the fresh cream.

Add the condensed milk.

Over a low heat, cook gently until the colour starts to change.

Mix the cream of tartar with a little water and add to the pan.

Beat with a wooden spoon, then add the chopped cherries, vanilla essence and the rum and beat again.

Pour the mixture into a 20cm (8in) greased, flat tin.

Spread evenly over the base and allow to set, but cut the mixture into squares before it sets entirely.

Ingredients

675g (1 ½lb) sugar
225ml (8fl oz) single fresh cream
200ml (7fl oz) sweetened condensed milk
1 pinch of cream of tartar
75g (3oz) chopped cherries
1 tsp vanilla essence
2 tsp rum

Bread and Butter Pudding

Ingredients

10 slices (8ozs) of white bread
55g (2oz) butter
600mls (1 pt) milk
4 egg yolks
85g (3 oz) caster sugar
½ papaya, diced
½ large mango, diced
1 oz candied peel
1 tsp nutmeg
1 tsp vanilla essence
2 tbsp sultanas

Method

Approximate preparation and cooking time 1 hour 15 minutes

Grease a 1.2 litre (2 pt) oven proof dish.

Remove the crust from the bread (optional).

Spread with butter and cut into quarters.

Arrange half of the buttered bread slices in the prepared ovenproof dish.

Sprinkle half of the papaya, sultanas, mangoes and candied peel over the top of the bread.

Place the remaining bread slices over the fruit and sprinkle the rest of the fruit over the bread.

To make the custard, put the milk in a saucepan and bring almost to the boil.

Whisk the egg yolks and the sugar in a bowl.

Pour in the warm milk, add the vanilla essence and nutmeg.

Pour the custard over the bread and allow to stand for 20-30 minutes.

Bake in a pre-heated oven 200°C for 40-45 minutes.

Mango and Papaya Delight

Method

Approximate cooking time 25 minutes

Place the sugar in a pan and heat until it's caramelized.

Then add the water and continue cooking and stirring until the sugar is dissolved.

Add the papaya and mango to the syrup and cook for approximately 3 minutes.

Add the nutmeg and vanilla essence and half of the rum.

Dissolve the vegetable gelatine in hot water then add to the fruit mixture.

Set aside and allow to cool.

In the bottom of a tall glass, crumble approximately 2oz of the sponge cake, and pour approximately 1 dsp of rum over the cake.

When the fruit mixture is cooled, spoon the fruit over the sponge then make another layer of cake on top of the fruit mixture.

Finish with fruit at the top of the glass.

When ready to serve, pipe a rosette of cream on the top and decorate with chocolate flakes.

Delicious!

Ingredients

½ papaya diced
½ large mango, diced
4 tbsp sugar
300mls (12fl.oz) water
½ tsp nutmeg
1 tsp vanilla essence
225g (8oz) sponge cake
4 tbsp rum
2pts veg. gelatine (thickener)
110g (2oz) milk chocolate flakes
110mls (4fl.oz) double cream, whipped

Jamaica Trifle

Method

Approximate preparation time 30 minutes

Break the ginger cake into a glass bowl, covering the base with it and sprinkle the rum all over the cake.

Drain the syrup from the mangoes and, keeping a few pieces back for decoration, spread over the rest of the cake.

Pour the made custard over the mangoes.

Put the bowl into the refrigerator.

Allow to cool and set.

Spread the fresh whipped cream over the set custard and flash across fresh cream your melted chocolate.

Ingredients

1 ginger cake
110ml (4fl oz) rum
1 tin mangoes
575ml (1pt) custard
575ml (1pt) whipping cream
2oz melted chocolate for decoration

Drunken Pineapple

Ingredients

1 small ripe pineapple
Rum to taste
3 tbsp brown sugar

Method

Approximate preparation time 10 minutes

Do not remove the leaves from the fruit!

Cut the pineapple into 3 sections, lengthways, slicing through the leaves.

Cut the flesh from each 'shell' in one piece, using a sharp knife and cut out the core.

Halve the flesh lengthways, then cut through crossways into bite-sized pieces.

Put the 'shells' into individual dishes, replace the flesh in a 'staggered' fashion, then pour a generous amount of rum over.

Sprinkle with brown sugar and 'flash' under a hot grill.

Serve immediately with ice cream.

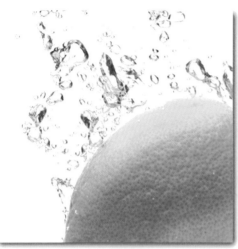

Beverages, Cocktails & Ice-cream

Classic Planter's Punch

Method

Shake all of the ingredients together.

Divide between 2 chilled tumblers.

Rest a long spoon on the surface of each drink and carefully pour 1 tbsp rum down the stem so that it stays on the surface.

Ingredients

170mls (6fl oz) dark rum
55mls (2fl oz) lime cordial or lime juice
3 tbsp caster sugar
dash angostura bitters
185ml (1/3pt) crushed ice

Frozen Daiquiri

Method

Liquidize all ingredients for 20 seconds.

Turn straight into chilled glasses and serve.

Ingredients

Serves 2
170ml (6fl oz) light rum
28ml (1 fl oz) lime cordial
425ml (¾pt) ice

Tropical Punch

Method

Pour the pineapple juice, orange juice, lime juice into a large punch bowl and add the sugar and stir until all the sugar is dissolved.

Add the chopped pineapple and melon pieces, the mint, rum and finally the ice.

Serve in a glass with some mint to garnish.

Ingredients

1 pt fresh pineapple juice
1 pt orange juice
150mls (6fl oz) lime juice
1 ripe mango, peeled and chopped
165g (6oz) white cane sugar
(or syrup)
110g (4oz) water melon, chopped
2 sprigs fresh mint, chopped
2 oranges, sliced and cut into quarters
1 pt white rum
Crushed ice

Aphrodisiac

Method

Put the soft brown sugar, evaporated and condensed milk into large bowl and whisk together until the sugar is dissolved.

Then add the nutmeg and continue whisking.

Add the vanilla essence and the ice and whisk together.

Add the stout and then finally the bottle of rum.

Serve in a long glass over crushed ice.

Ingredients

Serves 4-6
4 tbsp soft brown sugar
1 large can evaporated milk
1 large can condensed milk
4 tsp nutmeg
1 small bottle vanilla essence
1 bag ice, crushed
2 cans stout
1 bottle dark rum

Paw-Paw & Pineapple Kick

Method

Peel the paw-paw and pineapple, discarding the inner core and chop into small pieces.

Liquidize the pineapple and add the sugar and chopped paw-paw.

Place in a pan and over a low heat allow the sugar to dissolve. Do not boil!

Pour into an earthenware jug or container with a lid, and cover.

When cool, add the rum and stir well.

Serve with crushed ice.

Ingredients

Serves 10
6 paw-paws
6 pineapples
900g (2lb) granulated sugar
2pts rum
Crushed ice

Banana Shake

Method

Put all the ingredients into a blender. Liquidize until smooth.

If the consistency is too thick, just add a little more milk.

Taste, and if too sweet, stir in a little lemon juice.

Serve in a chilled glass.

Ingredients

Serves 1
275mls (½ pt) milk
1 large banana, not too ripe, peeled and roughly chopped
2 tbsp natural yogurt
1 tbsp clear honey
Pinch of nutmeg

Buttery Rum Toddy

Method

Put the cinnamon into a jug.

Add the rum and butter.

Pour on the boiling cider.

Stir well until the butter is dissolved.

Sprinkle with nutmeg and serve warm.

Ingredients

Serves 1
275ml (½pt) boiling cider
110ml (4fl oz) light rum
Knob of unsalted butter
2 tsp cinnamon or 1 cinnamon stick
Pinch of nutmeg

Knockout Orange

Method

Wash and thinly peel the oranges.

Squeeze the juice and strain to remove the pips.

Dissolve the sugar in the orange juice over a low heat, together with the peel. Do not boil.

Pour into an earthenware jug or container with a lid, and cover.

When cool, add the rum and stir well.

When ready to serve, remove the orange peel. Serve with crushed ice.

Ingredients

Serves 10
14 oranges (try to include at least 2 Seville oranges)
900g (2lb) granulated sugar
1.1l (2pt) rum
Crushed ice

4 O'clock Punch

Method

In a large pot or container, pour in the boiling water.

Add the tea and sugar.

Stir and allow to brew.

Strain and cool.

Combine the juices and ginger ale.

Stir well and add to the tea.

Serve with crushed ice and decorate with orange slices and mint leaves.

Ingredients

Serves 6
1ltr (2pts) fresh boiling water
4-6 tsp tea
110g (4oz) soft brown sugar
150ml (¼pt) lemon juice
275ml (½pt) orange juice
575ml (1pt) ginger ale
2 sprigs mint and orange slices
for decoration

Mango Smile

Method

Peel the mango and cut all the fruit away from the stone.

Place all the ingredients into a liquidizer and blend until smooth.

Whisk in the cream.

Pour into glass goblets; pipe a blob of cream on the top.

Garnish with a slice of mango and chocolate vermicelli.

Chill until ready to serve.

Paw-Paw or pineapple can be used as alternatives, but whatever you choose the taste is heavenly!

Ingredients

Serves 1
1 large mango
2 tsp vanilla essence
1 dsp coconut or banana liqueur
1 dsp caster sugar
225ml (8fl oz) whipping cream
Chocolate Vermicelli for
decoration

Sweet Tia

Method

Ingredients

Serves 1
50mls Tia Maria
50mls double cream
Chocolate curls for decoration

Mix equal quantities of Tia Maria and double cream.

Pour into a glass filled with crushed ice.

Sprinkled with chocolate curls. Yummy!

Jack In The Hat

Method

Shake all the ingredients together.

Divide between chilled tumblers.

Ingredients

1lb jack fruit
170ml (6fl oz) rum cream
190m (8fl oz) milk
185ml (1/3pt) crushed ice
Crushed ice

Egg-Nog

Method

Whisk the condensed milk, sugar and eggs together.

Add the lemon or lime and vanilla essence.

Finally, add the rum and mix in well.

Pour into glasses, sprinkle with nutmeg and serve with crushed ice.

Ingredients

Serves 6
4 x 425ml (¾pt) cans sweetened condensed milk
50g (2oz) caster sugar
6 medium eggs
Grated peel and juice of 1
lemon or lime
2 tsp vanilla essence
575ml (1 pt) rum
(or more, according to taste!)
1 dsp nutmeg

Ginger Beer

Method

Grate the ginger and the ring of the lime. Squeeze the juice of the lime, in a large saucepan, pour the sugar on top, add the water, ginger and cinnamon and stir together.

Cook on a low heat for 10-12 minutes. Allow to cool, strain the mixture, bottle and keep in a fridge ready to serve with crushed ice.

This is very refreshing!

Ingredients

4 litres water
7oz (175g) fresh grated ginger
3 limes, squeezed, keep the skins
12oz sugar
1 dsp cinnamon

Pina Banana
Method

Mix together and serve

Ingredients

Serves 4
2 large bananas, liquidized
170ml (6 fl oz) pinacolada mix
170ml (6 fl oz) milk
Crushed ice

Mango Flip
Method

Peel the mangoes, halve and discard the stones.

Blend the mango fruit with the other ingredients for 2 minutes.

Serve with ice.

Ingredients

2 large mangoes, peeled and chopped
175g (6oz) white sugar
110g (4oz) sweetened condensed milk
225ml (8 fl oz) rum
575ml (1 pt) orange juice

Cool Watermelon
Method

Chop the flesh of the melon and remove the seeds.

Liquidize with the other ingredients for 2 minutes.

Strain through a fine sieve and serve with ice.

Ingredients

Serves 4-6
½ large watermelon
110g (4oz) white sugar
170ml (6fl oz) strawberry cordial
225ml (8fl oz) vodka

Guava Juice

Ingredients

4lb ripe guavas
1½ lb light brown cane sugar
8pts water
1 lime

Method

Approximate cooking time 30 minutes

Wash and cut the guavas into small pieces.

Put the guavas into a heavy-bottomed saucepan and pour over the sugar.

With a wooden spoon mix the sugar and the guavas together.

Add half of the water and put on the heat.

When the mixture starts to boil, pour the rest of the water and the lime juice and the husk of the lime into the pan and simmer for a further 20 minutes.

Remove from the heat and put through a fine sieve.

Using a wooden spoon, push the flesh through as much as possible.

Scrape the back of the sieve and stir in the guava juice.

Allow to cool and serve in a glass with ice and a slice of lime.

Or put in a glass type container until ready to serve.

Delicious!

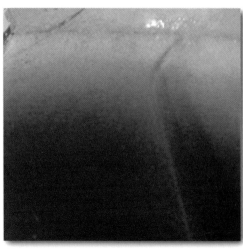

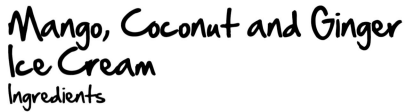

Mango, Coconut and Ginger Ice Cream

Ingredients

2 large mangos 450g (16oz), peeled and cooked in sugar and water
2 egg yolks
1 tsp cornflour
2 tsp water
3 dsp desiccated coconut
2oz (50g) crystallized ginger, chopped
2 tbs caster sugar
150ml (¼ pt) single cream
150ml (¼pt) double cream

Method

Heat the single cream in a saucepan until hot.

Do not boil.

Put the egg yolks in a bowl and add the cornflour.

Mix together adding the water.

Pour the hot cream onto the egg yolk, stirring continuously.

Pour the mixture back into the saucepan and using a whisk keep stirring until the mixture becomes a thick coating on the back of a spoon.

When this happens, pour into a bowl.

Allow to cool.

Purée the cooked mango in a blender until smooth.

Add the sugar to the double cream and whisk until soft peak.

Fold in the mango purée, the desiccated coconut and crystallized ginger.

Stir all the mixture together gently making sure they are all combined.

Pour all ingredients into a loaf tin or a shallow freezer-proof container.

Cover and freeze for 2½ hours or until half frozen and soft in the middle.

Put the mixture in a bowl and break up the ice cream with a fork and return to the container, cover and freeze until firm.

Put the container of ice cream in the main compartment of the fridge for approximately 20-25 minutes before serving, to allow softening.

Nutty Cream Freeze

Method

Dissolve the marshmallows and milk together over a low heat.

Add the rum essences.

Remove from the heat and allow to cool.

Fold in the whipped cream and nuts.

Spread the mixture out in a flat tray and freeze.

When half frozen, cut into squares.

Ingredients

275ml (½pt) milk
20 marshmallows
2 tsp rum essence
425ml (¾pt) double cream, whipped
175g (6oz) chopped nuts

Lucious Melon Ice

Method

Cut the hard skin off the melon. Remove as many of the black seeds as possible.

Cut the melon into small pieces, put in a liquidiser then strain through a fine sieve pressing through so that all the flesh can go through the sieve.

Scoop the flesh from the bottom of the sieve and put into the juice.

Stir altogether.

Place all the juice into a heavy-bottomed saucepan, add the sugar and put onto medium heat, stir and dissolve the sugar.

Cut the lime and squeeze the juice into the melon juice and place two halves of the lime into the mixture.

Cook for 4-5 minutes.

Remove from the heat and allow to cool. Pour the mixture into plastic containers or freezer bags so they can be sealed to prevent any juice seeping out.

Place in the freezer for up to 12 hours, then remove from the bags or the plastic containers and whisk with an electric whisk then put it back into the containers until ready to serve.

Using an ice cream scoop, scoop one or two small balls in a glass container and decorate with a small piece of mint.

Ingredients

3lb ripe water melon
1 ½lb cane sugar
1 lime

I hope you have enjoyed this book as much as I have putting it together.

I have to admit, during the making of this, I have met the most memorable people and have laughed from beginning to end.

I also hope that with these recipes and the information in this book, you have learned a little more about the Caribbean lifestyle and their ways of cooking.

Maybe one day you will take the opportunity to visit these amazing, tropical countries and sample the delights first hand.

Rustie

x